Los Angeles
Sep. 1968

THE LOGIC OF CHOICE

THE LOGIC OF CHOICE

AN INVESTIGATION OF
THE CONCEPTS OF RULE AND RATIONALITY

by

GIDON GOTTLIEB

London
GEORGE ALLEN AND UNWIN LTD
RUSKIN HOUSE   MUSEUM STREET

PRINTED IN GREAT BRITAIN
in 11 point Ehrhardt type
BY C. TINLING & CO. LTD
LIVERPOOL, LONDON AND PRESCOT

CONTENTS

I

INTRODUCTION

The *concept* of rule is shrouded in confusion and controversy. Yet rules are relied upon and used in a very wide range of fields: language, law, ethics, games and logic, to mention but a few. The *use* of rules involves an equally wide range of difficulties not the least of which is related to the notion of rationality itself. It is with the concepts of rule and rationality, with the use and application of rules and with the choices and decisions that they call for that we shall be principally concerned in this book.

Both the concept and the use of rules are embroiled in a series of fundamental controversies. Questions have been raised about the philosophical status of rules in the light of theories asserting the exclusive 'meaningfulness' of empirical and logical knowledge. These questions have arisen in connection with attempts to reduce legal rules to correlatives of observable human behaviour and in connection with attempts to exclude 'metaphysical' – factually meaningless – knowledge from legal and ethical theory. Moreover, questions about the status of rules have gained added urgency from the writings of the American and Scandinavian 'Realists'.

Other questions have arisen about the rationality of reasoning purporting to rely on rules for guidance. Commentators have indicated that such reasoning can be neither deductive nor inductive and that it certainly is not scientific. The implication has been that rule-guided reasoning is either not rational or that the concept of rationality itself requires fresh investigation. This implication may have played a role in the growth of an important new school of jurisprudence in Belgium which assimilates legal argumentation to a species of rhetoric.

Equally grave and far-reaching doubts have been expressed about the adequacy of theories of statutory interpretation and precedent which account for the use of rules in legal systems. These doubts have been accompanied by significant controversies about neutral and principled judicial decision-making which agitate observers of the American constitutional scene. At the same time an important scholarly debate has been pursued about the relative role of rules, purposes and policies in judicial processes and legal systems – a debate which raises fundamental questions specifically about international law and about constitutional issues. This is the debate which has been sometimes associated with a divergence of approaches attributed to the Harvard and Yale law schools.

Profoundly conflicting views have also been expressed on the relationship between legal and moral rules. Modern works on jurisprudence by Kelsen, Ross, Fuller, Hart, Goodhart and Devlin have all dealt with it. They are clearly marked by the rival positions of natural law and of legal positivism. Investigations of the concept of law have led to equally divergent positions which have not inhibited increasingly numerous behavioral studies of judicial decision-making. At the same time a shift has occurred in logical theory with the growth of deontic logic and the weakening of the analytic ideal. This shift raises the possibility of a future reconciliation between judicial and logical theory.

These arguments have taken place against the background of systematic doubts, both in legal and in ethical theory, about the possibility of choosing between competing sets of values and policies otherwise than upon subjective preferences; doubts which have had an impact on the theory and practice of adjudication. The philosophical background to these arguments includes the contempt of existentialist theories for the attempts to decide human problems with the guidance of generalized rules in disregard of the demand of authentic justice that each case be decided on its merits. This background includes however also the Wittgensteinian school of philosophical analysis which stresses the importance of linguistic usage for philosophical inquiry and which is more concerned with the investigation of normative concepts than either existentialism or empirical positivism.

This impressive web of philosophical and professional disputes is woven out of related controversies. It raises in its cumulative impact the deepest and most unsettling doubts about the philosophical credentials of the fields using or relying upon rules and laws. It has become difficult indeed to pursue the investigation of these controversies apart from a systematic inquiry into the concept of rule and the use and application of rules leading to a reappraisal of the yardstick of 'rationality' in terms of which we have been operating. With this end in mind we propose to discuss the questions just briefly alluded to in the course of the following chapters in the light of both legal and philosophical writings.

The exploration of existing controversies in the course of the structured investigation of the concept and use of rules is designed to lead to the elaboration of a number of independent conclusions. It is designed to lead to the revision of the prevailing concept of rationality, to the articulation of model standards for rational arguments – to lead in other words to a logic of rule-guided choices and decisions.

II

SOME NOTIONS OF
RATIONALITY AND LAW

*Reasoning with rules is not reducible to a species
of deductive reasoning*

Theories about judicial and moral reasoning can be meaningfully assessed in terms of concepts of logic. Yet while these theories have been changing, the concepts in terms of which they have been discussed – deduction, induction, rationality – have also undergone great modifications. As a result, analysis of legal and moral reasoning cannot be pursued in terms of stable and fixed conceptual standards. Such analysis requires the constant reassessment not only of the subject matter of analysis – legal and moral reasoning – but also of the fluctuating standards in terms of which investigation must necessarily proceed. It is as though we were trying to measure an object which changes size by employing a shrinking or expanding yardstick. This state of affairs evidently requires that equal attention be given both to theories of reasoning and to concepts of logic and rationality in terms of which they are discussed. We might otherwise be employing obsolete critical standards.

Theories on the relations between law and reason provide a flagrant instance of the havoc caused by inept tools of analysis. The history of the study of the function of reason in the judicial process is the story of an epistemological inferiority complex. Legal theory surrendered uncritically to the prevailing notions of rationality. The judicial process was successively disguised in a variety of attires to secure the appearance of conformity with respectable forms of analytic and scientific reasoning. Judicial reasoning was equated with deductive thinking comparable in its certainty to Euclidean geometry. It was later adorned with the trappings of scientific reasoning and was said to follow the successful method of physics and chemistry. It was also presented in the shape of pragmatism and was even put forward as an altogether non-rational process. In all the various appearances it was made to assume, judicial reasoning was anything but itself. Somehow it always eschewed accurate analysis and the tension between the judicial process and the instruments used to examine it remained too acute for the drawing of meaningful conclusions. The difficulty was well stated by Cardozo,

'Into that strange compound which is brewed daily in the cauldron of the courts . . . . ingredients enter in varying proportions. . . . The elements have not come together by chance. *Some* principle, however unavowed and inarticulate and subconscious, has regulated the infusion . . . . a choice there has been, not a submission to the decree of Fate; and the considerations and motives determining the choice, even if often obscure, do not utterly resist analysis.'[1]

Recent developments in the field of logic make possible a re-evaluation of the relationship between law and reason. The traditional treatments of this subject are of little help, for they reflect the vain attempts to do the impossible: to equate judicial logic with a species of either analytic or scientific reasoning. This is precisely why it is worthwhile to examine these attempts; they disclose the full measure of the force of the distorting models.

Law is the last of the disciplines to have freed itself from the belief that it is possible to adhere to the method of deduction from predetermined conceptions. In this respect, however, there has been a wide cleavage between legal theory and judicial practice. The practices of common law judges have never seriously suffered from the pull of theoretical models of right thinking. The common law has always displayed the peculiar English genius for institutional integrity. Whether out of laziness, out of insight bordering on genius, or out of sheer ignorance, common law judges never sought outside the law edification or directions about how they ought to reason or judge. On the contrary, they have always regarded with the greatest suspicion attempts to view the judicial process in terms of logic. The following statement of a High Court judge is not out of character,

'We have in England a deep distrust of logical reasoning; and it is for the most part well-founded. Fortunately, our judge-made law has seldom deviated into that path; but on some of the rare occasions when it has done so, the results have been disastrous.'[2]

It is not far in spirit from Holmes' famous dictum that the actual life of the law has not been logic, it has been experience.

On the continent of Europe, however, the pull of formal scholastic and Cartesian thinking has altered the course of legal history. Civil law is the product of men who have taken Greek geometrical models of reasoning as their criterion of rationality and who found in the Roman codes abundant stores of propositions. Civilian lawyers were as a rule better educated than their English opposite numbers and they found it harder to disregard the precepts of right thinking with which they had been brought up. By the time of Spinoza, the logic of deductive and formal thinking had captured the imagination of enlightened men. The code-makers of the eighteenth century sought the fundamental postulates from which all rules would logically follow. They expected that it was possible to anticipate new problems and they sought to arrive at agreed solutions before they arose. They believed with Bentham and Austin that a perfect code could be devised to govern all possible combinations of circumstances. Under the codes, they believed that everything that a judge need know, would flow from the godhead of reason, from the postulates.[3] Judicial discretion was to be done away with, and judges would merely act like subsumption machines. In the same vein, John Stuart Mill, in his *Treatise on Logic*, asserted that under a written code, the method of reasoning which a judge follows is wholly and exclusively a method of syllogistic reasoning.[4]

In the nineteenth century, mathematical modes of reasoning rather than geometric became the fashion among Roman law commentators. In Germany, Savigny and his followers the *Pandectists* adhered rigorously to the deductive model of reasoning in their 'juristic mathematics of concepts'. Their immense deductive skills were used to bridge the gap between the propositions of the Corpus Juris and the requirements of the industrial age. The story of the attack on the 'juristic mathematics of concepts' has been fully told. Many of the great names of jurisprudence are connected with it. Ihering, Gény, Ehrlich, Gmelin and Pound all contributed to the discredit of mechanical jurisprudence.[5] But optimistic remnants of nineteenth century deductivism still linger on. Proposals are now made to replace judges by electronic machines which would extrapolate the right decisions from the stored datum of legal propositions. These proposals must be carefully distinguished from other, more realistic projects to use computers for information retrieval. It is still often believed that in juristic thinking the problem lies in proper deduction rather than in a choice between competing propositions – a choice of which machines remain incapable.

Theories of logic have changed no less than legal theory. Shifts in such theories have had their echo in theories in other disciplines. In legal philosophy, deductive reasoning has been understood to mean that every case is governed by certain and unchanging rules, which preexist the decision of a case.[6] In philosophy, deductive reasoning is a term which has been reserved for arguments in which the major and minor premises positively entail the conclusion in the sense that to assert the premises and to deny the conclusions amounts to an inconsistency or contradiction.[7] It is a species of reasoning which cannot in its conclusion tell us anything not already stated in its premises. Ludwig Wittgenstein put the matter thus,

'6.1 The propositions of logic are tautologies.
6.11 The propositions of logic therefore say nothing (They are the analytical propositions).
. . . .
6.1222 . . . logical propositions can no more be empirically confirmed than they can be empirically refuted. Not only must a proposition of logic be incapable of being contradicted by any possible experience, but it must also be incapable of being confirmed by any such.'[8]

Logical implications do not depend on the truth of the premises, but are formal only. In the ancient example:

> Socrates is a man;
> All men are mortal;
> So Socrates is mortal.

we have an example of a deductive syllogism. The main philosophical objection to regarding legal reasoning as a species of deductive reasoning is that the heart of the question in legal reasoning is the classification of particulars. If one gives a term a certain interpretation, then a certain conclusion follows, but logic cannot help classify particulars. Logic thus cannot tell anything about the truth of the premises.[9] The following syllogism despite the falsity of its premises is no less valid than the syllogism about Socrates' mortality:

> Sparta is a democracy;
> No democracy has a King;
> So Sparta has no King.

It is always possible to formulate a major premise (rule) and a minor premise (facts) of a judicial syllogism so that it entails a necessary conclusion. But this conceals the fact that the hard problem in a legal decision consists in the adoption and formulation of such premises.

There is also another objection. In many cases competing major premises are advanced and it is not then possible to use syllogistic reasoning to determine which of the competing premises is the applicable one. Moreover, questions about the selection of the 'relevant' facts, which make up the minor premise, from the total situation in which a choice or judgment is required, cannot be resolved by reference to the deductive syllogism. Nor can questions about factual situations not contemplated in the major premise of the syllogism such as questions involving novel factual circumstances be deductively resolved by resort to premises antecedent to such circumstances.

It has also been pointed out that the attempt to reduce reasoning with rules to a species of deduction can lead to decisions which do violence to the requirements of justice which is itself one of the purposes of legal reasoning. Such reasoning may then become self-defeating, hence irrational. This attempt also tends to give the impression that in all cases the rule applied preexists the decision of a case – an impression frequently contradicted by historical evidence. Nevertheless, the theory that judicial decisions in code systems are founded on deductive reasoning has had remarkable staying power. We still find in a 1951 edition of a major work on legal theory that,

'His decision [the judge's in a codified system] is deduced directly from general to particular – from the general legal rule to the particular circumstances before him.'[10]

It is significant that this statement was changed in a subsequent edition of the same work. The philosophical objections summarized here suffice to establish that reasoning which relies on rules for guidance – whether legal rules or other rules – is not reducible to a form of deductive reasoning.

Reasoning with rules is not reducible to a species
of inductive reasoning

Despite authority to the contrary, reasoning with rules is not reducible to a species of inductive reasoning any more than it is reducible to a species of deductive reasoning. According to C. K. Allen, however, the theory of English law starts with the object of finding the general rule applicable to the particular case. But it does not conceive of the rule as being applicable directly by simple deduction – which is allegedly the case in codified systems. Allen maintains that where the French judge has to find his master principle in formulated propositions of abstract law, the English judge has to search for it in the learning and dialectic which have been applied to particular facts and that he thus always reasons inductively.[11]

Another leading jurisprudential text, Paton on *Jurisprudence*, is in agreement with Allen in this respect. Paton argues that since the attempt to reduce law to a definite number of legal rules and to make the judicial task one of pure deduction has failed, a reaction has set in. The judge, he writes, is not always able to find his general principle ready-made; frequently it may be implicit in a line of cases and the utmost subtlety may be necessary to discover it. Hence, according to Paton, the worship of induction has become popular.[12]

The term induction has been bandied about by legal philosophers as frequently as that of deduction. Induction has attracted much attention from both philosophers and logicians and it has now acquired a fairly settled meaning. Two kinds of induction are generally differentiated. Kneale distinguishes between primary and secondary induction; between induction which refers to reasoning in which universal propositions are established by consideration of instances falling under them and that which refers to the reasoning which establishes an hypothesis. For, according to Kneale, the essential feature of such an hypothesis is that it relates observables of a certain kind to some other things which are not observable.[13]

Braithwaite describes induction as the inference of an empirical generalization from its instances, or of a scientific hypothesis from empirical evidence for it.[14] Support for an inductive conclusion is not absolutely perfect since it involves reasoning from what Strawson calls one non-necessary statement to another, that is – in which the first does not entail the second.[15] Inductive conclusions have a degree of probability attached to them, but they are never absolutely certain. This connection between the concepts of probability and induction has long been recognized. In deductive arguments there are no degrees of entailment but in inductive reasoning the support for conclusions may be less than overwhelming and the probability of the conclusions changes accordingly. Wittgenstein expressed this thought very clearly,

'. . . . It is clear that there are no grounds for believing that the simplest course of events will really happen.

6.36311 That the sun will rise to-morrow, is an hypothesis; and that means we do not *know* whether it will rise.

6.37 A necessity for one thing to happen because another has happened does not exist. There is only *logical* necessity.'[16]

Inductive conclusions are indelibly connected to 'observables' and to the universe of empirical discourse. Any 'facts' may, therefore, form the subject matter of induction. It is thus possible to study the past decisions of courts with a view to formulating propositions about the disposition of cases which may provide a basis for the prediction of future decisions. Significantly, some behavioral studies of the decisions of the U.S. Supreme Court which claim to have predictive value make no reference to legal rules or principles at all.

It is, moreover, quite impossible to reach a moral or legal decision inductively since the ground of support for such a decision – the applicable rule – cannot be assimilated to empirical evidence and since the decision cannot be characterized as either probable or improbable. In other words, it is not possible to *apply* a rule inductively, irrespective of the manner in which that rule may be derived. Conclusions in legal and moral decisions are based upon legal or moral rules and not on raw empirical evidence. Even when the authority for a decision is tenuous its binding force is the same as in a case in which the decision is backed by the strongest possible authority. Legal decisions admit of no differences of degree; they are all equally binding. While inductive reasoning is designed to govern inferences about matters of fact, reasoning relying on rules is designed to guide decisions and judgments. To pretend that inductive reasoning can guide the making of judicial decisions overlooks the objection that induction can be used only when the observables and the propositions under which they fall are beyond our power to change. The borrowing of the language of natural science to describe normative processes serves merely to blur irreducible distinctions between separate universes of discourse.

Reasoning with rules is not reducible to a form
of scientific reasoning[17]

Since the late nineteenth century some legal philosophers have tried to demonstrate that legal reasoning is but a branch of that fashionable mode of reasoning: scientific reasoning. This attempt was prompted by influences similar to those that led to the induction theory of judicial reasoning. Legal philosophers often failed to disentangle theories about the scientific method from theories about Aristotelian induction which had currency at the time. As Paton points out there arises today an emphasis on the logic of discovery and the drawing of an analogy between the task of the judge and that of the natural scientist. It is argued that the judge frames a provisional rule to deal with a particular case; in further decisions the formulation of the rule is tested by application to new facts and may be adapted, modified or rejected until finally the rule appears in a satisfactory elaboration.[18]

The pull of scientific models was felt early in legal history, and it was neatly expressed in one of Holmes's more famous dicta that,

'The prophecies of what the courts will do in fact, and nothing more pretentious, are what I mean by the law.'[19]

This dictum was echoed by Walter Wheeler Cook who wrote that,

'We as lawyers, like the physical scientists, are engaged in the study of objective physical phenomena. Instead of the behavior of electrons, atoms or planets, however, we are dealing with the behavior of human beings.'[20]

Law and the natural sciences were believed to be identical, except for those necessary variations due to the change of subject matter. There is little doubt that legal theory reflected the position expressed by Wittgenstein in the *Tractatus*, where he stated the positivist conviction that while logic and mathematics are tautological – that is, say nothing about the world – natural science is the only field in which it is possible to say something 'meaningful'. This led him incidentally to assert that his propositions in the *Tractatus* are senseless, and to end that period of his life with the proposition 'Whereof one cannot speak, thereof one must be silent.'[21] Faithful echoes of this position are found in the legal literature of the first half of this century. The following excerpt from the *Yale Law Journal* of 1929 is characteristic,

'Mathematics is the enterprise having for its aim to establish hypothetical propositions. Science is the enterprise having for its aim to establish categorical propositions. The two enterprises together embrace the whole knowledge-seeking activity of man.'[22]

Legal philosophy, like other disciplines was faced with the difficulty of fitting into this dichotomy. It was sufficiently insecure of its own epistemological grounds to be dominated by the scientific method. This submission entailed the redirection of the objects of legal philosophy, focusing attention on those elements of the judicial process which are empirically verifiable; that is, on observable behavior rather than on the more elusive application of rules. Jurisprudence thus tended to become a specialized branch of sociology.

The scientific study of law is unquestionably a legitimate mode of inquiry. The only danger to the knowledge-seeking activities of jurisprudence lies in viewing legal *science* as the only valid alternative to a 'pure' theory of law seeking the formal relationships between norms and juristic concepts. The passage just cited shows the reality of this danger. But this danger certainly does not warrant the repudiation of the scientific study of law. Shifts of methodology are often accompanied by manifestations of exclusiveness; new methods, not unlike new religions, often claim to be uniquely qualified to discover 'the truth'. Thus, though the findings of legal science are of great interest, the literature on legal epistemology must not succumb to the messianism inherent in the move to a new method.

Although sociological jurisprudence has good claims to be counted among the social sciences there are major objections to equating legal with scientific reasoning. In recent years, the scientific method has been the object of considerable philosophical inquiry notably by Karl Popper, who rejects the equation of science with the empirical or inductive method. This latter method, although it appeals to observation and experimentation, nevertheless fails according to Popper to live up to scientific standards. Popper objects that astrology, for example, with its stupendous mass of empirical evidence based on observation, could properly claim to use inductive but not scientific procedures. He suggests instead that the proper demarcation line between scientific and other theories is their falsifiability or refutability or testability.[23] Now as Paton already observed, objective experiments cannot be resorted to for testing the correctness of judicial decisions. Indeed, whether we adopt Popper's demarcation line between science and pseudo-science or the empiricist test which it displaces, it is clear that reasoning with rules is manifestly non-scientific. There is nothing testable about a decision, for the consequences which it may occasion can themselves be evaluated only in non-empirical terms. Nor can a rule or principle be tested in subsequent applications for there again the assessment would turn upon non-empirical considerations. The concepts of testing, experimenting, or verifying in induction and scientific procedure refer only to situations in which the proposition tested cannot affect the empirical evidence. Where there is no objective empirical datum, testing in the strict sense is impossible. The claim that a judge applies a rule scientifically is, therefore, strictly speaking meaningless.

Irrationalist theories of the judicial process

A full account of models for the judicial process would have to include a review of some theories which have not been mentioned so far: J. Austin's treatment of analogical reasoning, C. S. Peirce's theory of abduction and J. Dewey's logic of judgments of practice. There are, moreover, a number of important contemporary developments: the revival of rhetorics by Ch. Perelman, the creation of deontic logic by von Wright, and many-valued normative analysis by Bobbio as well as the work of Wasserstrom.[24] A critical discussion of these theories lies, however, beyond the province of this work. But, it is clear that neither J. Austin, C. S. Peirce nor J. Dewey succeeded in formulating a model for reasoning with rules capable of replacing the deductive-inductive models of traditional logical theory. John Dewey's theory was probably the most influential of the three. He believed that the legal process invites a reconsideration of the traditional views about logic itself. He argued that either logic must be abandoned or that it must be a logic relative to consequences rather than to antecedents, a logic of prediction of probabilities rather than one of deduction of certainties. This logic, which was closely tied to what he called the logic of judgments of practice, suggested that reflective valuation was a realistic alternative to deduction and to induction.[25] Dewey had diagnosed the difficulty accurately but failed to articulate a method for the assessment of competing sets of probable consequences that would flow from alternative contemplated decisions – assuming apparently that some outcomes were clearly more 'desirable' than others. His emphasis on ends-in-view pointed out realistically that hard choices of value are not always imminent or inevitable. He optimistically refrained from dealing with hard cases.

The rejection of the deductive theory of judicial decision has led many writers to commit what Wasserstrom calls the irrationalistic fallacy.[26] These writers, according to Wasserstrom, assert that most of the important problems which arise in the decision of cases must be settled by the courts in an arbitrary fashion *because* they cannot be settled by reference to the canons of Aristotelian logic. It would seem however that Wasserstrom underestimates the distress of the critics of the deductive theory who found that the alternative inductive and scientific theories of judicial decision failed them as well. These critics were then left without *any* models of rational inference which they could have preferred to theories assimilating legal reasoning to feeling, emotion, sensory experience or unanalysed personal predilection.

The disenchantment with the ideals of analytic and scientific reasoning was total. Not surprisingly irrationalist theories of judicial decision gained currency. J. C. Hutcheson, Jr. suggested that a hunch or intuition of what is the just solution for a particular case is the effective determining factor in a judge's decision. In a similar vein, Oliphant argued that courts are coerced by an intuition about the fitness of the solution to a problem.[27] Jerome Frank also believed that the judicial process is not truly rational and that judges merely rationalize the desired results. In *Law and the Modern Mind*, he argued that the personality of the judge is the pivotal factor in law administration, and that decision varies with the personality of the judge who happens to pass upon any given case.[28] Another legal scholar, Stoljar, maintained that a judge's emotional reaction to the facts of a case determines the outcome. Stoljar, Oliphant, Frank and Hutcheson were thus all agreed that rules of law do not and cannot determine the outcome of cases however heavily they appear to be relied upon in opinions cited in support. Their work saw the withering of the significance of the concept of rule and its reduction to a mere rationalizing device.[29] Such theories about the nature of judicial reasoning coupled with the deepening awareness of the gulf between law and logic have led according to Llewellyn to a growing crisis of confidence in the U.S. appellate bar. Imbued with the businesslike postulates of early positivism, educated lawyers find their loyalties torn between their commitment to reason which compels them to conclude that judicial decisions must in important cases be arbitrary or subjective and between their faith in the courts as instruments for the impartial administration of law.[30] It is probable that this crisis will continue so long as the judicial process cannot be shown to meet the demands of widely shared standards of rationality and impartiality.

Ideals of rationality

The failure of the models of rationality in theories of the judicial process is significant for all forms of reasoning with rules. The objections about the relevance of the deductive, inductive and scientific models of reasoning for the application of legal rules arise from the character of rules as such. Irrationalist theories of the judicial process, which have their counterparts in ethical theories such as Emotivism, cannot be displaced as long as no revised and attainable rational ideal is articulated. This in turn requires an analysis of the concept of rationality.

The mutual interaction of model procedures and of the standards by which they are judged is common to many fields. In physics, for example, Professor Oppenheimer discussed a similar problem arising ouf of Niels Bohr's theory of complementarity. He said that,

'The basic finding was that in the atomic world it is not possible to describe the atomic system under investigation in abstraction from the apparatus used for the investigation by a single unique objective model. Rather, a variety of models, each corresponding to a possible experimental arrangement and all required for a complete description of possible physical experience, stand in a complementary relation to one another, in that the actual realization of any one model excludes the realization of others, yet each is a necessary part of the complete description of experience in the atomic world.

It is . . . not yet fully clear how characteristically or how frequently we shall meet instances . . . in other fields, above all in the study of biological, psychological and cultural problems.'[31]

Such difficulties are also echoed in the perceptive comments of I. A. Richards writing about the study of language,

'Let me begin with a doubt, a pervasive and penetrating doubt – truly a bosom doubt. It concerns the language to use in these or any other remarks about language.

The very instruments we use if we try to say anything which is not trivial about language embody in themselves the very problems we hope to use them to explore. The doubt comes up, therefore: how far can we hope to be understood – or even to understand ourselves – as we use such words? And in the lucidity of this doubt the literature of this subject can take on a queer appearance. Must confidence be in inverse ratio to the security of its grounds?

This situation is not, of course, peculiar to the study of language. All studies suffer from and thrive through this. The properties of the instruments or apparatus employed enter into, contribute to, belong with and confine the scope of the investigation.'[32]

This is the same kind of problem which must be faced in the use of 'rational' standards for the analysis of 'rationality.'

Logicians have traditionally equated the concepts of rational and valid reasoning. Validity was conceded only to arguments conforming to the analytic syllogism. Strictly speaking, the concept of validity has application only to individual analytic arguments or forms of analytic arguments. Arguments conforming to the analytic syllogism were marked 'deductive' and 'conclusive' while non-analytic arguments were marked 'inductive' and 'inconclusive'. Formal validity was just what logicians wished to be universally possible.[33] Descartes had maintained that it is proper to consider as false all matters about which it is possible to doubt. In *Règles pour la Direction de l'Esprit* he postulated that the certainty of mathematics is the ideal of all knowledge.[34] Hume, in the *Treatise on Human Nature* also believed that the only arguments 'conformable to reason' were those which come up to analytic standards.[35]

This concept of valid reasoning is also at the root of the so-called problem of induction. Evidently, all inductive processes are by deductive standards invalid since the premises never entail the conclusions. Undeniably, as Strawson points out, inductive processes are crucial in the formation of beliefs and expectations about matters which cannot be directly observed. The difficulty with induction arises when an 'invalid' argument is taken to be an 'unsound' argument, and an 'unsound' argument one in which *no good reason* is produced for accepting the conclusion. Accordingly, if inductive processes are invalid, if all arguments produced in support of non-deductive conclusions are unsound, then we have no good reason for relying on any of these conclusions. This, of course, is repugnant to common sense. But, as Strawson and Toulmin recently pointed out, when the demand for justification arises in this way, it is in effect the demand that induction shall be shown to be really a kind of deduction; for nothing less will satisfy the doubter 'when this is the route of his doubts'.[36]

The attempts to justify induction by analytic standards has failed. The upshot of this failure has been a reassessment of the very demand to justify induction. It has been seen that what often lies behind such a demand is the absurd wish that induction should be shown to be some kind of deduction, or more precisely, that it meet the demands of the analytic model of reasoning. The other sense which could be given to the demand is in the form of a request for proof that induction is a reasonable or rational procedure and that there are good grounds for placing reliance upon it.[37]

This way of looking at the justification of induction led to the dismissal of the whole problem. The failure of induction in terms of the analytic model does not spring, it has been said, from a weakness in the arguments, but from the nature of the problems with which they are designed to deal. Analytic criteria are accordingly simply irrelevant. The impasse reached in the attempt to justify induction has thus led to the abandonment of the analytic ideal.

Such abandonment has far reaching implications in logical theory. It implies that if the function of logic is not to judge arguments by reference to their conformity to the analytic ideal, arguments must be assessed by reference to some other standard. Instead of one ideal form of reasoning there must be a plurality of standards which good arguments must meet. Logic must instead be concerned with the soundness of claims we make in different fields.

Theories about the role of logic are shifting accordingly. Friedrich Waismann argues that the application of logic is limited in an important sense; that the known relations of logic can only hold between statements which belong to a homogeneous field of discourse. In other words, that logic is concerned with the necessary relations between the concepts used in a particular discipline and the necessary implications of procedures adopted. This view leads to a many-level-theory of language in which 'every sort of statement has its own sort of logic'.[38] Gilbert Ryle's plea for an informal logic in *Dilemmas* is made in the same spirit. Ryle rejects the exclusive hold of formal logic on logical theory since it gives 'weapon drill in only a limited variety of rather short-range inference-weapons.'[39] Problems remain where questions of legitimate or illegitimate inference arise in everyday and technical discourse, and an informal logic is required to deal with the questions ignored by formal logic. Urmson has suggested giving a new meaning to the concept of validity. His argument is that the attempt to discuss the question of validity by means of an argument from standard examples is misconceived and leads to the dismissal of genuine philosophical questions. There are two important problems: 'what are the criteria for the validity of arguments in a given field' and 'why do we employ these criteria'.[40]

These developments were influenced by Wittgenstein's *Philosophical Investigations* in which he abandoned the position he had held earlier in the *Tractatus* that the propositions of logic say nothing since they are analytical propositions. In the *Investigations* he understood logic to mark the limits of the language game. In the *Investigations* he compares the multiplicity of the tools in language and of the ways they are used with what he had said earlier in the *Tractatus* about the structure of language.[41] The function of logical laws, in the *Investigations*, is to serve as standards and rules.[42] Implicit in the *Investigations* is the assertion that reasoning about language is rational without being either analytic or scientific. J. O. Wisdom also rejects the inductive-deductive dichotomy of logical forms and points to legal argument as an example of a distinct logic which is at the foundation of both induction and deduction.[43] Strawson, in his painstaking discussion of two kinds of logic indicates the limited use of formal logic. He outlines the argument later developed by Toulmin that all that could be asked of 'induction' is that it be shown to be a rational rather than an analytic procedure. In the *Uses of Argument* Toulmin articulates the plea for a new role for logic more fully than his predecessors. In his view, the failure of non-analytic reasoning to conform to the analytic ideal does not stem from a lamentable weakness in the arguments, but from the nature of the problems with which they are designed to deal. He writes that,

'In logic as in morals, the real problem of rational assessment – telling sound arguments from untrustworthy ones, rather than consistent from inconsistent ones – requires experience, insight and judgment, and mathematical calculations . . . . can never be more than one tool among others of use in this task.'[44]

In brief, the test of analycity (of strict, necessary entailment) must give way to tests of validity and rationality for arguments and procedures in a given non-analytic field. The concept of 'field of argument' thus acquires new importance. The rejection of the analytic ideal, the suggestion that every sort of statement has a logic of its own, that law has a logic of its own, the emphasis on the separateness of distinct levels of discourse, all point to the 'field dependence' of non-analytic arguments. This notion can be traced all the way back to Francis Bacon who wrote in the *Novum Organum* that

'Next comes another diversity of Method, namely that *the Method*

used should be according to the subject matter which is handled.
For there is one method of delivery in the mathematics (which are
the most abstracted and simple of knowledges), another in politics
(which are the most immersed and compounded). And (as I have
already said) uniformity of method is not compatible with multi-
formity of matter. Wherefore as I approved of Particular Topics for
invention, so to a certain extent I allow likewise of Particular
Methods for transmission.'[45]

The concept of a field of argument is intimately related to the
applicable concepts of validity and rationality for these are themselves determined in terms of such a field. It is not always easy
to characterize an argument as belonging to this or that field
or to determine the limits and boundaries of a given field, since
alternative characterizations of a field are possible. In connection
with moral and legal reasoning, for example, it is possible to
look upon judicial and moral decision-making as the appropriate field, or upon choosing or upon decision-making in
general.

We define our field as the field of reasoning in which reliance is
put on rules for guidance. This permits the construction of a
rational model of arguments for following or applying rules in a
variety of contexts. This determination of the field of argument
fastens on *rules* as the critical inference-guidance device to be
analyzed. The concept of a field of argument leads to another
concept, to a field dependent model of rational arguments. If the
concept of rationality is a function of the boundaries of a field, and if
it indicates the applicable concept of validity, it becomes then necessary to elaborate a model procedure for the assessment of the
rationality of arguments *in* such field. The model of rational arguments thus fulfils in rule-using fields the functions which the inductive model performs for inductive reasoning.

When we referred to deduction, we were clearly not merely
speaking of the validity of arguments *in* deductive systems, but
referred also to the validity *of* deductive systems. In the same way
we referred not only to justification procedures *in* induction, but
also to the justification *of* induction. Similarly, here we must distinguish between the justification and rationality of arguments using
rules and between the justification and rationality of the model in
terms of which we can assess such arguments. We thus use a three-
layered concept of rationality:

1. specific arguments *in* a field, the rationality of which is assessed in terms of

2. a model procedure for reasoning in that field, which performs in such field the functions which the model of inductive reasoning performs for inductive arguments, and such model is in turn

3. justifiable in terms of general notions of rationality.

Evidently, the model of reasoning with rules assumes particular significance if it is accepted that it also relates to the *rules* of inference for reasoning in various contexts. For example, on the view that logic is but a set of rules of inference the model would apply to logic itself.

The displacement of the criterion of analytic consistency is fraught with dangers. Since it is possible to speak of the 'rationality' of substantive arguments without reference to their formal or analytic validity, there arises the possibility of a plurality of right procedures in different fields of inquiry. But unless this change is going to be the signal for an anarchy of loose critical standards, rigorous tests of rationality must obtain where the test of analycity is discarded. The great danger in works which demonstrate the irrelevance of the analytic ideal lies in leaving the door open for the unchecked proliferation of new critical standards. Such proliferation is likely to occur wherever no serious model procedures of reasoning are elaborated to take the place of the displaced analytic ideal.

To take a specific example, the justification of the method of the natural sciences, which is sometimes confused with induction, has not in modern times rested on the unattainable ideal of analytic certainty. Ever since Hume's *Treatise*, it has been widely recognized that the certainty of mathematics is out of the reach of the natural sciences. Radical empiricists like Ayer have instead justified the method of the sciences by reference to its 'success', by reference to the empirical verification of its propositions, 'We trust the methods of contemporary science because they have been successful in practice'.[46] Yet Popper has convincingly argued that empirical verification and success in practice are by themselves inadequate for the characterization of an investigation as scientific. By these standards astrology and biblical prophecies might qualify as sciences. This has led to the problem of the demarcation of science, and similar demarcation problems arise in other non-analytic fields.

The autonomy of the canons of rationality in different fields poses, as we have seen, the problem of devising workable models of reasoning for the 'liberated' fields. In the absence of such models the job of evaluating arguments in fields like law and morals cannot be done.

They would then be evaluated only in terms of their success in persuasion. Assessment in terms of effective persuasion would reduce legal and moral arguments to a genus of advertising. 'Sound' legal or moral arguments would then resemble good advertisements – they would be those that persuade best. There is little doubt that in the final analysis the failure to design a rational model in lieu of the displaced analytic and scientific ideals, would consecrate the devaluation of legal and moral argument to a species of rhetoric, often less effective than advertising.

If, indeed, the proper function of logic is to tell sound arguments from unsound ones, rather than analytic from inconsistent ones, then rational standards must be designed in a way which would make this possible. Certain characteristics required of a model for reasoning guided by rules can thus be discerned:

a. The model must furnish a guide or a manual so to speak, for the *process* of drawing inferences with rules in fields in which rules are used such as law and ethics. Hence, such a model cannot merely reflect patterns of argument in common use. Comparisons between such patterns and the model cannot, therefore, be used to assess the model. On the other hand, there must be sufficient correspondence between habitual patterns of argument and the model if it is to be applicable to arguments which recognizably belong to these fields. There is bound to be *some* correlation between the model and forms of argument.

b. The validity of the model cannot be assessed in analytic or empirical terms. The validity of the model is constituted otherwise. It hinges upon the necessary connections between the logically distinct ingredients which are involved in reasoning with rules, such as facts and purposes, which cannot be ignored when rules are utilized to direct reasoning. The model must at every point reflect the necessary recurrent relationships between these elements. These necessary relationships provide the inexorable basis of the model.

c. The model must set the highest relevant standards of reasoning to which it is possible to aspire. The model should indicate a necessary procedure for the impartial and objective application of rules. The necessary patterns of argument can be used as a yardstick for measuring the quality of deliberation. Any deliberation which intends to be as rational as possible must necessarily conform to the ineluctable patterns of argument and relationships of the model. Failure to do so can only lead to distortion, to a pretense that

deliberation with rules does not necessarily involve certain relationships which the model discloses to be necessary.

The model marks a departure from the neat form of the syllogism.
In order to express the connections between the elements present in
legal and moral deliberation, it is presented in a rather rambling
form. It is considerably more complex than the traditional syllogism.

III

THE LOGIC OF
REASONING WITH RULES

Some concepts of rule

J. L. Austin remarked that we do not have to go very far back in the history of philosophy to find philosophers assuming more or less as a matter of course that the sole legitimate business of any utterance – that is of anything we say – is to be true or at least false.[1] In recent times things have changed. The 'verification movement' was concerned to find out which things are true or false – leaving the matter to be decided by empirical observation – and which are just nonsense. More recently, philosophers began to ask whether after all some of those things which, when treated as statements of facts, were in danger of being dismissed as nonsense, did really set out to be statements of facts. The 'use of language' movement has now made it clear that there are a multitude of uses of language which are not utterances which report situations truly or falsely but which are nevertheless interesting, legimate and meaningful.

Sentences guiding all sorts of decisions and actions are foremost among such uses of language. They are normally couched in the form of rules and precepts. Ryle observes in the *Concept of Mind* that such sentences have often been interpreted as being categorical reports of particular but unwitnessable matters of fact, and this has led to the identification of the mental with the 'ghostly'. Thus rule sentences, Ryle says, belong to the class of 'dispositional statements'. They neither report observed nor observable states of affairs. But their jobs are closely connected with actual occurrences for they are intended to apply in particular situations. Like any other dispositional statements, the statement of a rule – or a law-statement – does not embody the report of any actual event or occurrence, it does something else,

'A law is used as, so to speak, an inference-ticket (a season ticket) which licenses its possessors to move from asserting factual statements to asserting other factual statements. It also licenses them to provide explanations of given facts and to bring about desired states of affairs by manipulating what is found existing or happening. Indeed we should not admit that a student has learned a law, if all he were prepared to do were to recite it. Just as a student, to qualify as knowing rules of grammar, multiplication, chess or etiquette, must be able and ready to apply these rules in concrete operations, so, to qualify as knowing a law, he must be able and ready to apply it in making concrete inferences from and to particular matters of fact, in explaining them and, perhaps also, in bringing them about, or preventing them. Teaching a law is, at least *inter alia*, teaching how to do new things, theoretical and practical, with particular matters of fact.'[2]

Ryle does not refer only to regularities expressed in law statements characteristic of the natural sciences. However, in the case of positive or moral laws, it is perhaps more apt to speak of such laws as, so to speak, *inference-warrants* rather than inference-licenses. For the inferences which such prescriptive laws contemplate are generally not merely licensed but are required and obligatory.

The notion that rules of all sorts function as guidance devices is gaining recognition among philosophers influenced by Wittgenstein. He pointed out in the *Investigations* that rules function not unlike sign-posts designed to direct mental operations. He observed that when we look to rules for instructions, we do something without appealing to anything else for guidance. This analysis is reflected in Hart's discussion of the 'internal aspect' of rules.[3]

The study of the function and structure of rules marks a significant departure from traditional treatments of non-scientific laws and norms as a species of imperatives. The imperative theory, notably as elaborated by Hare in the *Language of Morals*, justifies the application of general principles of logic to sentences in the imperative mood, which include a variety of norms and commands. It focuses on sentences of a recognized grammatical mood, and of a definite linguistic structure. It must not be confused, however, with the imperative theory of law advanced by J. Austin nearly a century ago which defines laws and rules properly so-called as a species of commands.[4] Hare's imperatives are studied from the viewpoint of the language of morals which he equates with prescriptive language, while the Austinian imperatives are studied as social phenomena. This analysis, on the other hand, disregards the forms and kinds of *linguistic* utterances. In view of the breakdown of grammatical criteria it concentrates on the role and function of rules and of statements which, when reduced, expanded or analysed into their standard forms, perform rule-functions. This change is required because imperative sentences are not exclusively used as norm formulations and because all norms cannot be formulated by means of imperative sentences. As von Wright points out in *Norm and Action*,

'... norm-formulations, linguistically, are a very varied bunch. They cut across several grammatical types of sentences without including or being included in any one type. One must therefore warn against the idea of basing the conceptual study of norms on a logical study of certain linguistic forms of discourse.'[5]

It is the use and not the form or look of the sentence or expression which indicates whether it is a rule statement, and it makes little difference at this juncture whether we refer to rules, law statements or to norms. In other words the notion of rule or norm *function* determines the character of a statement rather than the form in which it is couched.

This analysis of the function of rules and laws makes it possible for example to dispose of some of the difficulties inherent in regarding a legal concept like 'corporation' as a peculiar species of episodic statements which refer to unobservable events and occurrences. The nature of legal concepts is very specific and it illustrates the characteristic task of rules. That this is so, is a modern discovery. Under the sway of positivist doctrines which classify sentences as either logically true (analytic) or false (contradiction) factually true or false or merely emotive,[6] it was difficult to situate legal terms like 'marriage' or 'corporation'. This kind of positivism has led to bizarre comparisons between legal and mystical concepts. The positivistic doctrinal straightjacket led Hägerström to write,

'This insuperable difficulty in finding the facts which correspond to our ideas of ... rights, forces us to suppose that there are no such facts and that we are here concerned with ideas that have nothing to do with reality. ... Thus it is shown that the notions in question cannot be reduced to anything in reality. The reason is that ... they have their roots in traditional ideas of mystical forces and bonds.'[7]

In his celebrated inaugural lecture at Oxford, H. L. A. Hart challenged the validity of the dichotomy of 'reality' and 'fiction' with regard to a legal term like 'corporation'.[8] Legal terms, he asserted, are not descriptive in the sense that they correspond to existential phenomena which exist apart from the system of legal rules. Nor are they fictional for they are capable of referrring to actual events. They are terms peculiar to normative systems, to systems in which facts and decisions are connected by imputation and relevance. Such terms represent a concise formulation of normative statements. They are, in other words, but shorthand formulations of rule statements. They are the creation of a normative system. To take an example, a 'contract' is a legal term, a normative statement, which can be reduced to the formula, 'When X is then Y ought to be'. This formula does not refer to the existence of a contract, but specifies under which conditions a 'contract' will be created. When I say that there is a contract, I am not only saying that there is a rule which specifies under which conditions a contract arises. I also assert that these conditions have been met; I assert the existence both of a legal rule and of the facts contemplated in the rule (note the different meanings here of 'existence'). The statement that a 'contract' exists is neither a statement of fact nor a statement of rule. It is neither a purely empirical statement nor a purely hypothetical one. It is a statement of mixed law and fact, a normative statement. Similarly, a 'checkmate' in chess is neither a mere statement of the fact that I have moved my pieces on the board so as to trap my opponent's king, nor is it a mere hypothetical statement, for something *did* happen on the chessboard to which I allude when I speak of a 'checkmate'. 'Checkmate', like 'contract' is a normative statement which explains the conditions under which the statement, 'I have checkmated him' is true, and which indicates how to draw conclusions from moves on the chessboard.

This dual role of normative concepts is confusing. A 'checkmate' or a 'contract' is – depending upon its role in the particular case – either an operative fact (protasis) or a resulting fact (apodosis). It is an operative fact when the consequences of its existence are disputed, and it is a resulting fact when its existence is questioned. If in a game of tennis, my ball lands on the boundary mark, the question may be 'is my ball out?' And this question can then be answered by reference to the rule which provides for just this sort of contingency. On the other hand, in the question, 'What happens if my ball is out?' the term 'out' then appears as the given of our inquiry, while in the previous question it is the point in issue. Normative terms like 'out' have a dual function: they enable us to test whether the circumstances which they contemplate have arisen, and they enable us to determine the consequences of such circumstances.

In normative formulation this can be stated as,

Rule 1. 'When a contract is broken then damages ought to be paid,' or 'When a contract is broken, then Y ought to be.'

Rule 2. 'When there is an agreement for consideration then there is a contract,' or 'When X is then there is a contract'. The agreement for consideration is then the operative fact.

H. L. A. Hart's analysis marks the emergence in logic of terms proper to normative systems which do not bear the characteristics of scientific descriptions or of analytic statements. With this clarification legal science is finally liberated from a futile controversy between rival schools of thought, some asserting that a 'corporation' is a fictitious thing, some that it has an objective reality, and some that legal terms are mere tools for the prediction of the behaviour of judges and other officials.

There are a number of concepts like rule, norm, law and precept which all license or warrant inferences. These concepts are related and there is no strict English usage for discriminating between them. They are often used interchangeably. There is a complicated network of similarities overlapping and crisscrossing between them; sometimes overall similarities, sometimes similarities of detail. Such similarities are evocatively characterized by Wittgenstein as 'family resemblances'.[9]

One of these similarities is that rules and norms generally – to which we here refer as normative statements – are devices for the guidance of *mental processes* of inference – whether conscious or otherwise – leading to decisions, actions, attitudes, judgments, choices, conclusions and the like. It is this overall characteristic which expresses the principal function of normative sentences which provides the foundation for much of this analysis. Viewed in this light, the concept of rule is not as mysterious as H. L. A. Hart suggests.[10]

Max Black observes that while commanding and promising are relatively well demarcated activities, there is no correspondingly well demarcated activity associated with rules and norms. The concept of rule is versatile in a way that 'command' and 'promise' are not.[11] It is, however, unnecessary to discuss in detail the various kinds of normative sentences. It is sufficient for our purposes merely to refer to the most prominent species:

i. laws of nature – natural laws like the law of physics known as Snell's law;

ii. laws of logical and mathematical reasoning – these are laws like the law of the Excluded Middle;

iii. laws of the state and other positive authorities – these are laws like the Civil Rights Act of 1964;

iv. rules of a game – these are rules like the rule of chess that one one may not 'castle' after a 'check';

v. rules of grammar – these are rules like the rule that the words 'would' and 'should' can be used in indirect speech after a verb of saying, thinking or believing in the past;

vi. prescriptions and regulations – like the 'no smoking' regulation in a university library;

vii. rules of practice and customs – like the social custom of rising when a woman enters a room;

viii. technical directives and recipes – like the recipe for Canard à l'Orange;

ix. moral rules – like the rule that one ought to keep one's promises.

By now the functional kinship between legal and moral rules is apparent. Both sets of rules steer ratiocination leading to decisions and choices between alternatives. This identity of purpose suggests a methodological unity between legal and moral reasoning. These should be distinguished, however, from the numerous other processes equally directed to reaching decisions and judgments which are not guided by rules such as those leading to managerial, political and economic decisions which are free from the overbearing dictates of preexisting rules. Reasoning with rules – both legal and/or moral – involves similar yet logically distinct ingredients. In both cases deliberation arises out of an actual set of *events*, which gives rise to a situation in which a *choice* or a *decision* is required. Both types of reasoning are governed by *rules* or *examples*. In both the rules and examples must be applied through a *process of reasoning*, which may require a consideration of the *interests* and *purposes* or policies which the rules are designed to promote, and in both instances questions about the proper role of choice between purposes and policies are in order. On the other hand, the methodological unity of the field of reasoning with rules must not obscure the significant differences between judicial and moral decisions, which we need not, however, enter into at this point.

The structural characteristics of rules

The problem of demarcation between legal and non-legal rules in no way impinges upon the other facets of this analysis. Legal, moral and other prescriptive rules maintain constant structural characteristics. Just as a knife, in order to function as a knife, usually consists of a handle and a blade, so a rule is constituted of distinct component parts. These parts are necessary for the rule to function as a rule. They are functional requisites of rules in the same way that blades are functional requisites of knives. The principal components are:

1. an indication of the circumstances in which the rule is applicable;

2. an indication of that which ought, or may, or must be, or not be, concluded or decided;

3. an indication of the type of inference contemplated, whether under the rule it is permitted, required or prohibited;

4. an indication that the statement is indeed designed to function as a rule or inference-warrant.

The first element – the pointing to the circumstances in which the rule is applicable – covers the whole range of situations envisaged by the rule itself for triggering off, so to speak, its own application. These circumstances may be identified in terms of the time, place and persons to whom the rule is addressed, or they may be indicated in terms of other rules yet, upon which they may depend. For example, the rules governing matrimonial domicile apply to married persons, but the existence of a state of marriage is itself dependent upon yet other rules. We refer here to this element of a rule as its operative part or *protasis* (strictly speaking this term means an introductory clause expressing a condition).

The second element which we mention – that which the rule seeks to attain – can in practice mean a great many things. It could mean a decision, a choice, an expectation or an attitude to be adopted. In all cases, however, that which the rule seeks to accomplish is something as to which a human being normally has an alternative. It is pointless to provide by rule for something which is bound to happen anyway, for example, to stipulate that 'breathing is compulsory'. Where things are physically necessary, rules have nothing to accomplish (we speak of the law of physics, but not of the rules of physics). This second element is here referred to as the *apodosis* of a rule (strictly speaking, the consequent clause of the conditional sentence).

The third element – the type of inference or mental operation contemplated – is often identified by the word 'ought' or 'may' or 'must' or 'shall' and the like. It indicates the *character* of the rule, that is, the character of the inference-warrant itself. We need not here go into the peculiar debate surrounding the nature of many of these words, like the word 'ought'. What matters is that the rule identify whether the inference contemplated is permitted, required, prohibited or otherwise. This element is the *character tag* of a rule.

The fourth element – an indication that the statement is designed to function as a rule – arises out of the peculiar fact that rules, as we have already noted, cut across several grammatical types of sentences. They are a varied lot indeed. It is impossible by merely looking at a statement to determine whether it is designed to be acted upon as a rule. It is often necessary to look at the total setting of the statement in order to determine the matter. A 'no smoking' sign in a theatre is directed to the audience, but a similar sign in the set on stage is probably part of the décor. Sometimes the language of a statement is ambiguous because its function is concealed by the grammatical mood used. Thus the sign 'trespassers will be prosecuted' is not in the imperative mood. Someone not familiar with English might even think that it is a prediction. The linguistic form of a statement discloses little about its function. The utterances 'drivers, stop' and 'workers, unite' have a lot in common from a grammatical viewpoint, but surely this is inconsequential.

The structural characteristics of rules are not, therefore, evident from a study of their form. When we say that rules have an inherent internal structure we refer to ingredients which they must possess in order to be able to function as rules. Although these ingredients are not always detectable by a mere perusal of the rule statement, this does not mean that they are merely fictional attributes of rules. Any utterance which is designed to function as a rule *must* have the potential of being reduced, expanded, analysed or translated into a standard form such as 'in circumstances X, Y is required/permitted'. Any statement which cannot be so restated cannot function as a rule for it will inevitably fail as a tool for guiding the drawing of inferences. Normative utterances need not, therefore, be completely formulated. The crucial question about such an utterance, from a functional viewpoint, is whether it lends itself to a *restatement* in normative form.[12]

At this stage of the argument, an aside may be permitted. Wittgenstein has repeatedly emphasized that grammar is a set of rules for the use of language analogous to the rules of a game.[13] Hotly controverted questions arise however also about the components of the language game. It would seem that the very words and concepts of a language are themselves rule-like. That is, they embody instructions as to the circumstances and purposes for which they may be used, in much the same way that technical directives and recipes do. Words behave as the basic particles of all languages which represent galaxies of rules for the use of words, or microrules so to speak. These micro-rules have the internal structure of technical directives and they can each be restated in the form of utterances broadly like 'in circumstances X, and for purpose Y, it is English to use the word Z'. If words are rule-particles, so to speak, then every form of human communication may well be a type of normative activity which displays some of the characteristics of reasoning with rules. This point is itself suggested by Wittgenstein's comment that,

'. . . we talk about it [the phenomenon of language] as we do about the pieces in chess when we are stating the rules of the game, not describing their physical properties.

The question "What is a word really?" is analogous to "What is a piece in chess?" '[14]

The internal structure of rules does not indicate *all* the conditions which must be satisfied for a rule to operate as a rule. For rules to do their job as rules, it is also necessary to keep in mind as Fuller points out in *The Morality of Law* the circumstances in which they would fail altogether as guides for action.[15] Such failure can occur if the rules are not made available to those whom they are supposed to direct or if they are promulgated so that they cannot possible direct action (in many instances, however, retroactive rules merely instruct the attachment of future consequences to past action). Moreover, obscure or vague rules, no less than obscure road signs or faded maps, fail as tools for guidance. They evidently fail also when there are clearly contradictory rules or rules which it is impossibe to follow. (It is not always clear to whom a rule is directed; the imposition of strict liability for some kinds of activities is really tantamount to a direction to courts and other officials to allocate liability for injury in a certain fashion; it is confusing to assume that these rules are merely directed to influence the behaviour of those who may be held liable.) Fuller also mentions rules that are known to change so frequently that it is hard to use them for orientation. He also refers to cases of failure of congruence between rules as announced and their actual administration which would give rise to severe doubts about their very standing as rules. One might also perhaps add rules of such complexity (is this just an instance of obscurity?) that it is impracticable to expect those to whom they are directed to be able to use them.

Since rules are devised as tools for the introduction of order and recurring patterns, they must be distinguished from particular commands addressed *ad hominem*. This is a problem which pre-occupied John Austin who makes much of distinguishing *general* commands from particular ones. It underlines one of the basic functions of rules: to guide reasoning to like conclusions in like situations.

It is possible to look upon principles as a species of large scale rules which cannot be applied with the same accuracy and certainty as ordinary rules, since both the circumstances in which they are applicable and the measures to which they point are of general character.[16] But scale in mapping as in rule-making is a function of purpose, so that rules which might operate quite satisfactorily in one context may be too broad or loose in another. Nevertheless, the utility of principles lies in their constituting easily recognizable reference points in galaxies of complex rules. So that while they may not furnish firm guidance in concrete cases they do at least suggest the topography of the terrain for required action. They stand in the same relationship to rules as continental maps to area maps.

The correspondence between rules and events

When we speak of reasoning guided by rules, we have in mind the use of rules in specific situations. Since rules are used to guide inferences they do not operate at large. Like other linguistic tools, they are resorted to only when the occasion so demands. *Rules presuppose a context of application*, a relationship with such context. The nature of this relationship is apparent in the analysis of decisions by resort to chance.

Rules are not the only device for guiding inferences. There may be, for example, no rule to govern a decision on a tied vote. The decision may then be taken by drawing lots.

The choice between the many devices for guiding decisions – rules, votes, chance – depends on a variety of factors: whether the decision is judicial, managerial or personal, whether it is feasible to vote, etc. Thus courts of law use rules to make comparatively simple decisions: to award or deny a remedy, to find an accused guilty or to acquit him. They act in concrete cases, where the parties are few and the alternatives limited. They can use rules to guide their decisions. Without getting involved in the question of justiciability, it can be observed that not all kinds of issues lend themselves to reasoned decision; not all kinds of cases are appropriate for adjudication; and not all kinds of differences can be resolved by a vote. Which player shall play white in a game of chess may best be decided by drawing lots; which airline shall be entitled to fly on an additional route may best be decided by a non-judicial body; and which judge shall sit on a case may best be decided otherwise than by a vote.

However, as we observed, every device for guiding a decision *can be restated in the form of a rule*: 'the candidate polling a majority of the votes cast shall be elected' or 'the person drawing the white King shall play white'. It is always possible to reduce even a decision by resort to chance to a formulation in rule form. When a dispute about the return of a book is settled by tossing a coin, the mode of settlement can be restated in normative terms: 'The person who calls tails, ought to keep the book'. Formally, there is no difference between a decision reached by resort to chance and a decision founded upon some other rule. Both types of decision are determined by statements which can be formulated in rule form. Thus the statement that he who borrows a book ought to give it back is not formally different from the statement that he who calls tails keeps it. Both statements can be reformulated: 'in circumstances X, Y is required'.

What is then the difference between drawing lots and the use of rules – legal and moral – for guiding decisions? The essential difference seems to lie in the nature of the facts which both types of devices take into consideration. The outcome of drawing lots depends on matters unconnected with the total situation in which the decision is required – the fall of a coin. The outcome of a decision determined by legal or moral rules is on the contrary heavily dependent upon such situation. The difference rests in other words in the relationship between the *protasis* of a rule – that part of the rule which points to the circumstances in which it operates – and the situation which calls for the decision. This relationship involves two separate but related matters: the *correspondence* of the situation to the *protasis* of a rule and the selection of the *relevant* aspect of such situation. Thus, when the dispute about the return of a book is settled by tossing a coin, the rule adopted – tails keeps – is entirely divorced from any question about whether the book was borrowed or promised in the first place. The inference required by the rule that 'tails keeps' is almost automatic. The disposition of the case turns on 'heads or tails' and on no other consideration. The decision is then not a decision of *that situation* at all. We are then not really using a rule to guide us *in* that situation, but merely to *get* a decision unconnected with it. We are then not really reasoning with a rule, but going through a simulacrum of such reasoning. Reasoning with a rule requires that we allow ouselves to be guided by a rule when we want to reach a decision in a given situation. It requires that we be guided *in that situation*.

Trials by ordeal, by battle, and by divination have this in common: the actual facts or events of the case are divorced from the protasis of the rule applied. Or to put it in another way, the factual 'is' and the normative 'ought' are entirely unconnected. Legal fictions illustrate this point clearly. When fictions are used, the facts that are formally taken as the basis of the decision have little or no relation to the actual events in the case. In such trials the judge or the jury find facts which they know to be at variance from the truth. They do this in order to obtain a certain result. The fiction is entertained as a means of achieving a desired end. In trials by chance no particular result is contemplated. The desired objective is a decision of some sort. On the other hand, when fictions are used there is a real if covert link between the actual events in the case and between the *protasis* of the legal rule which is applied. But this link is not between the formal *protasis* and the actual events, but with the *de facto protasis*. In such cases a revised rule is in practice applied in lieu of the rule which appears to be applied, and there is then a *de facto* nexus between the facts and the rule, or in other words, between the 'is' and the 'ought'. For example, in England grand larceny was punishable by death until the early nineteenth century. The theft of property valued at forty shillings or more was grand larceny. Juries often refused to send to the gallows people whose only crime had been a small theft: they refused to apply the existing law. They sought to substitute for the law on the books another more lenient law. This was done with the aid of fictions. Thus in the 1808 case of *R. v. Macallister*,[17] a jury found a £10 Bank of England note (£10 = 200 shillings) to be worth only 39 shillings. The jury, without apparent disrespect for the law on the books, applied another law by means of the fiction about the true value of the banknote. The *formal* finding of fact of the jury bore little relation to the actual facts of the case. Macallister had stolen £10 (or 200 shillings), but the jury applied the rule governing thefts of less than forty shillings. The *protasis* of the rule applied by the jury bore little resemblance to the actual theft; in practice the jury had altered the law. What lies then behind the fiction reveals the inherently reasoned character of the decision. The apparent irrationality is only a cover for the application of a new rule.

In every legal decision a link is established between the actual events in the case and the *protasis* of the applicable rule. But this link is often imperfect. For example, I drive my car into the park to pick up a wounded person, I am then prosecuted for breach of a regulation which excludes all vehicles from the park. In this case, there is some connection between the operative part of the regulation invoked against me and the actual circumstances which led to my prosecution. The correspondence is between the operative part of the regulation, the *protasis*, 'Anyone driving a vehicle into the park' and the fact that I did drive a vehicle into the park. But there is also a clear discrepancy between a *full* account of the events in the case and the facts noticed in the *protasis* of the regulation. A full account of the case would be more complex than the *protasis* of the 'no vehicles' rule suggests. Though I admittedly did drive a vehicle into the park, I did so with the intent of assisting an injured person, and this additional fact, which is part of the complete account of the case, is not referred to in the *protasis* of the regulation. In this case, therefore, the correspondence between a full account of the events and the operative part of the applicable regulation is only partial. The rule applied does not really contemplate this kind of situation. Not all the *relevant* facts are taken into account by the rule used to decide the case. And to the extent that part of the relevant background of the case is ignored, the decision tends to resemble decisions taken by resort to chance. This would be an instance of the mechanical use of the rule, that is, an application in which the only correspondence that matters is between the formal protasis of the rule and between the events contemplated in it. The use of an inappropriate rule leads to misconceptions about the facts of a case. In our example, a mechanical use would suggest one question only, 'Did the accused drive a vehicle into the park or not?'. No other question would affect the outcome of my trial. All the facts not contemplated in the rule are simply irrelevant. The theoretical foundation of this method rests in the deductive view of legal reasoning according to which rules are deduced from one another, and facts are simply subsumed under them. But mechanical interpretation really resembles trial by chance in that the *protasis* of the rule may touch only marginally upon the central issue of the case. Puffendorf's famous case of the surgeon who drew the blood of a patient in the streets of Bologna is to the point. The surgeon was prosecuted for having operated in the streets, an act punishable by death under a statute which made public bloodletting criminal.

Mechanical interpretation avoids the question of how the rule of law comes to have a bearing upon the case in the first place; how does a rule for the preservation of public safety apply to a surgeon saving a human life when the surgeon in no way endangers this safety.[18]

Mechanical interpretations of this kind severely curtail the scope of judgment and reasoning. Decisions of this nature, are not actually taken on the basis of actual events but on the basis of fortuitous events which are of marginal importance only. Complete rationality is preserved only when the actual events and the events which are contemplated in the rule or rules applied coincide. If they diverge, interpretation is at best partly rational. It then lies half way between trial by chance and rational choice.

The first test of the rationality of a decision is then the *correspondence* between all relevant facts and the *protasis* of the applicable rule or rules. (It must be noticed that some of these facts may correspond to the *protasis* of rules pleaded in defense only.) This correspondence cannot, however, be absolute. All rules are necessarily a generalization which links similar situations for the purpose of decision. They are an attempt to marshall the variety and richness of experience into manageable categories for the purpose of guiding decision. The *protasis* of a rule must necessarily be more general than the facts of the case. Every existential situation is, strictly speaking, unique. The operative facts of a rule cannot be on all fours with an actual existential situation without losing their utility for further applications. There is, therefore, a constant tension between the facts of the case and the operative facts as stated in the rule. The demand of the particular situation is ideally to base the decision on all the relevant existential circumstances. The demand of any normative system – such as the legal system – is to base the decision on features that are relevant not only to the particular situation but which are also significant in other similar situations. The correspondence between a full account of the events and the operative facts of the rule is strained by the conflicting requirements of generalization and of individualization. But, in every decision, this correspondence must be established. The uniqueness of every situation is respected only in the Far Eastern cultures which do not seek the guidance of rules for the solution of disputes. We are told that in Confucian Chinese theory the resort to norms and codes is regarded as morally evil,[19] and that the process of settling disputes is more akin to mediation and no fact or event can be dismissed as irrelevant. Thus everything connected with the personal history of the litigants, and the unique circumstances of the case, is taken into account. Nothing is deemed immaterial if it has a bearing on the litigants and on the dispute between them. It is only in a system which does away with rules altogether, that it is possible to avoid the problem of the correspondence between the *protasis* of a rule and the relevant facts of a case.

The presupposition of context inherent in the concept of rule thus throws light on what is meant by the 'applicable rule'. It indicates that rules should be used only in circumstances which happen to correspond to the context for which they are designed (a question which is best dealt with separately in connection with 'purpose' and 'policy'). To use them in other contexts, in the name of fidelity to rules, is a gross misconception of their functions.

Language in rules

The operative parts of rules, which point to the circumstances in which they are applicable are often inordinately 'vague'. Now, this vagueness does not always arise as a consequence of poor or clumsy drafting. The difficulties in vague rules are not peculiar to adjudication or decision making; they are inherent in all language. In every language there is some tension between words and fact situations. As T. S. Eliot wrote,

> '. . . Words strain,
> Crack and sometime break, under the burden
> Under the tension, slip, slide, perish.
> Decay with imprecision, will not stay in place,
> Will not stay still.'[20]

The mathematician Friedrich Waismann has analysed the nature of *empirical* terms used in the sciences and their relevance to verifiability. His conclusions are very suggestive. He draws attention to the 'essential incompleteness of empirical description'. This incompleteness is one of the reasons for the 'open texture' of empirical terms (Porosität der Begriffe).[21] It makes it impossible to define empirical terms exactly as opposed to geometric terms like 'triangle' which can be defined completely. We never can be quite sure that we have included in our definition everything that should be in it; we can always make our definitions more detailed, more specific. The level of generality on which the facts are stated can always be questioned, and every definition, in Waismann's words, 'stretches into an open horizon'.

He also points out that however we limit the term we use, there is always some direction in which the concept has not been defined. Even if we take a notion as specific as that of 'gold', which is defined in chemistry by reference to its characteristic spectrum, it is still possible for this definition to be incomplete. Waismann asks, 'what if a substance were discovered which looked like gold satisfied all the chemical tests of gold, while it emitted a new sort of radiation?' It is quite inadequate to say that such a thing could not happen, for it might conceivably happen, and this alone shows that something can always arise which shall force us to change our definitions. A new situation can arise with new discoveries which would throw a new light on our interpretation of certain facts, and it can arise in the wake of some totally new experience which we cannot even imagine now. It is our inability to anticipate events and experiences, no less than our inability to give full descriptions of empirical occurrences, which makes for the constant defining and refining of our terms.

The open texture of empirical concepts requires some sort of decision when the meaning of a word is in doubt. When ordinary words are used in legal rules, and when there is doubt about the use of the word-in-the-rule we are faced with a very different kind of problem. The decision on the meaning of the word-in-the-rule is not just a decision about linguistic usage; it is a decision whether to apply the rule or not, and it often seems as if legal decisions involve questions of classification. Whereas the meaning of a word in common usage is settled by reference to its overall role in language, the meaning of the same word when it occurs in a rule may well be settled by reference to legal principle. It becomes a question of the application of law. It is, therefore, possible for the ordinary and the legal meanings of the same word to diverge. Much adjudication turns on questions like this, 'is a flying boat a ship for the purposes of an insurance policy? and for the purposes of property law?' And the answer to these questions will be governed by reasons different from those that govern the answer to the question, 'is something that is in all respects like gold but which emits different radiation, gold?'

Open texture must not be confused with vagueness. A term is vague when it is used in a fluctuating way. Vagueness can be remedied up to a point, but up to a point only. The word 'vehicle' is vaguer than the word 'automobile', but even the word an 'automobile' can be vague for my purposes when it is given in reply to an enquiry seeking to establish who damaged the right fender of my car. It is somewhat like the question of the right size for a screwdriver; it all depends on the size of the screws I am working with. Words must be adapted to the job they are supposed to do. The use of a vague word is like the use of too large a tool; it may have been adequate on another job. An atomic nucleus is a particle in atomic physics, and the sun is a particle in astronomy. It all depends what we are doing with the word 'particle'. Vagueness is, therefore, always a question of degree; it can never be 'vanquished'. Open texture then, is something like 'the possibility of vagueness.'[22]

IV

THE FACTS

Some concepts of fact

Rules are applied to facts. What these are is one of the vexing questions of philosophy, but one which, mercifully, we need not discuss. All that is required here is the articulation of criteria which direct the selection of facts material to the application of rules; their selection, that is, from the vast storehouse of available facts. This is a limited task, which enables us to skirt the debate on the nature of truth, the doctrine of logical atomism and the fashionable theories on perception. In saying that rules apply to facts, situations, and circumstances, and that they presuppose some *context* of application, it is permissible for our purposes to adhere to unrefined common usage of the word 'fact', particularly since we are not concerned here to distinguish between issues of 'fact' and issues of 'law'.

What then is this factual context for the application of rules? Is it constituted of the total fact situation in which rules are used? Evidently, the answer to this question cannot be, 'yes'.

We have seen that a full correspondence between all facts of a situation and the *protasis* of a rule cannot exist in a normative system in which a rule necessarily displays a considerable degree of generality. There is another more perturbing reason for the discrepancy between rules and facts. This reason lies in the very nature of giving accounts of occurrences.

Legal choice and judgment are made not on the basis of raw facts, but on the basis of an account or description of an event. Stuart Hampshire stated the problem in this fashion,

'The word "fact", here as always, is treacherous, involving the old confusion between the actual situation and the description of it; the situation is given, but not the "facts of the situation"; to state the facts is to analyse and interpret the situation. And just this is the characteristic difficulty of actual practical decisions, which disappears in the textbook cases, where the "relevant facts" are pre-selected.'[1]

Before choice, judgment or deliberation can take place, some selective intervention occurs, which picks out of the actual total situation some facts worthy of attention and deliberation. I say 'selective intervention' because it is the job of every account or description to seize upon some features of an occurrence as worthy of attention, and to exclude others as immaterial or distracting. Any description and any account is in this sense necessarily selective. For whatever is said, much more could have been said. Any account or description of 'what actually happened' necessarily depends upon some implicit or explicit standard of relevance. The problem of reproducing reality was clearly stated by Camus in his Nobel prize acceptance speech,

'Let us then be realists. Or rather, let us try to be such, if it is only possible. For it is not certain that the word has a meaning, it is not certain that realism, is possible, even if it is desirable. Let us first ask ourselves if pure realism is possible in art. To believe the statements of the naturalists of the last century, it is the exact reproduction of reality. It is to art what photography is to painting: the first reproduces when the latter chooses. But what does it reproduce and what is reality? Even the best photography is after all not a sufficiently faithful reproduction, nor is it yet realist enough . . . [the artist] frankly recognizes that one cannot reproduce reality without making a choice and rejects the theory of realism as it has been formulated in the XIXth century. It remains for him to find a principle of choice, around which the world will become organized.'[2]

That any account or description of an occurrence is already an interpretation has also been deftly observed by I. A. Richards,

'. . . to a much greater extent that we profess we communicate through offerings of CHOICES, not through presentations of FACT. Our statements of fact themselves must be buoyed up, if they are to float at all, on invitations of consent to CHOICES of meaning.'[3]

Judgment, decision and deliberation are then based on interpreted situations. Facts are not simply 'given', they are the outcome of a process of selective interpretation. For example, in the story of the rescue in the park, there are things left unsaid. Should it be noted that it all happened on the morning of February 3rd? That I wore a grey suit? Should it be reported that the temperature was 39° and that a pigeon sat on top of Garibaldi's bust? Is it irrelevant that a green car was driven north just as I was entering the park, or that a girl listened to music on a transistor radio? An electrician might have seen a wire dangling from the rear light of the car; a friend from the museum might have noticed the ugly pink of the red cross, and a student of mathematics, that the registration number added up to 13.

There are always more reportable things than reported facts. The difficulty does not lie in the need to select facts. Indeed, without some selection, we might never reach the stage of deliberation. We would be swamped by endless, massive descriptions – impressionistic, scientific, medical, historical, visual, auditive, in the style of the contemporary French novel – and all these descriptions might be 'true' that is, conform to what was observed to happen. But reaching a decision in good time, is of the essence of sound reasoning. Aristotle observed that,

'One man may deliberate too long, another not long enough. Here again we have not yet got the quality [of good deliberation] in its completeness. For that quality is correctness of deliberation, on the subject of what is advantageous, arriving at the right conclusion not only in the right manner but at the right time.'[4]

There is clearly then a need to isolate some distinct uses of the word 'fact' and to indicate in outline some distinctions other than that between the facts of a situation and a description of it. To recapitulate, this word is used to denote:

1. an occurrence, an event, process or state of affairs which can form the subject matter of a description,

2. what a witness retains or notices from what was there to be perceived,

3. the account of a witness,

4. the part of the testimony admitted by a court under the rules of evidence,

5. the facts considered to be material in the process of applying a rule to the facts.

One of the significant facets of 'the facts of a case' has been superbly dealt with by the fact-sceptics who directed their astringent criticism to the vagaries of testimony and credibility. Judge Frank, in *Courts on Trial* wrote,

'The facts of a case, remember, are not what actually happened but, at best, what the trial court says it thinks happened. For decisional purposes, the facts are therefore "subjective". They consist of the personal, individual, reactions of the trial judge or jury to the testimony of the witnesses. As I observed earlier, the formula should be, not

R × F = D
nor R × OF = D (i.e. objective facts)
but R × SF = D, (i.e. subjective facts. In this example R stands for rule, F for facts and D for decision).'[5]

The emphasis laid by the fact-sceptics on the subjectivity of belief in testimony is clearly connected with their concern for certainty and predictability. In the prediction of court decisions, the datum for making a forecast is the pattern of relationship between actual decisions and actual cases. Such a pattern can be upset if the courts base their decisions not on objective but on subjective facts. It then becomes even more difficult to meet the demands of scientific prediction.

The correspondence between material facts and the operative facts of legal rules depends upon the authenticity of the material facts themselves. If the view which the court takes of the total setting of a case is mistaken – or downright wrong – then the rationality of its decision is impaired. The decision is then based on a hypothetical situation which exists only in the mind of the court. Obviously a defective mode of proof can impair the rationality of an inference by falsifying the actual circumstances of the case. But a defective mode of proof does not impair the rationality of the process of reasoning *on the basis of the facts proved and believed*. And this is precisely where our interest diverges from the interest of the fact-sceptics. They are concerned with the proof of facts – with evidence. We are concerned with the rationality of reasoning on the facts proved and believed. Both aspects of the question are vital to decision-making.

This leads to another point. Relevance is spoken of also in the context of the proof of facts. In the law of evidence, relevant facts are those which throw light on the existence or the veracity of facts in issue, they are 'facts relevant to facts in issue'. This notion of materiality must not be confused, however, with the notion of material facts or of relevance which concerns us here. Giving birth to the facts is one thing, and dealing with them once they are established is another. The issue of the materiality of facts is unavoidable even when no doubts whatever are cast upon the credibility of witnesses or the truth of assertions made. It is an issue, which must be met even in the face of the best and most undisputed facts.

Standards by which facts are relevant:
(*i*) *The applicable rule*

In returning to the question of the facts material to a decision, it is easy to succumb to the assumption that materiality is, so to speak, something emerging out of the facts themselves, a feature *of* the facts. It is important to note that what is meant here by relevant or material facts is neither part of the inert episodic account or testimony – which forms the passive substance in which decisions must be made – nor part of rules applied in making such decisions. Material facts are a step in the *process of applying* rules to facts. They are the facts rendered material in such application. They are the facts chosen to be material. This is a distinction we shall explore in the next chapter, but what must already be noticed here is that materiality is neither to be found in the factual situations which are the presupposed context of rules nor in the rules themselves. The selection of the material facts is a process which itself presupposes standards to select the facts which ought to be treated as material from among the amorphous mass of the other facts which can be ignored.

Game analogies of the legal system have enjoyed a lasting vogue. The differences between games and law are however no less revealing. They disclose the separate nature of facts in games and in law. In a game like chess the only relevant facts of the game are the facts referred to in the *protasis* of the rules of chess. If White drops his pipe and accidentally alters the position of Black's queen, the change in the queen's position is not a 'move' in the game; it does not count. As Waismann has observed, the rules of a game of chess enable us to describe the whole game move by move, from the beginning to the end, and to describe the game *completely.*[6] Completely, that is, from the viewpoint of the game but not from the viewpoint of a narrative of what happened during the game. For example, the following moves are part of an account of the game: 'White played 1. B–K8, whereupon Black resigned since he has not means of averting the threat of 2. R×P ch, P×R; 3. B×Kt ch, Q×B; 4. Q–Kt8 mate.' The rules of chess select the significant events in the game *a priori*. It is entirely out of place to add to this account of the game that 'White ordered a lemonade'. The conditions for a move in the game are both necessary and sufficient; no checkmate can be defeated by a new or unforeseen contingency. The moves in chess are *constituted* by the rules, they are defined by the rules. Yet not everything in a game is circumscribed by rules. As Wittgenstein observed, there are no rules 'for how high one throws a ball in tennis' or how hard; yet tennis is a game for all that and has rules too.[7] To insist in a legal case that the only facts which matter are those contemplated in applicable rules of law suggests that if there were no legal rules at all then there could be no material facts either. Such insistence is founded on a misconception of the role and nature of law. Adjudication is not a game; it is a means for settling disputes which do not depend upon the existence of prior conventions, and which arise, for the most part, independently of legal rules. Some legal disputes are much more like disputes in a game than others. Thus disputes involving the law of negotiable instruments usually involve fact situations wholly defined by legal rules. But these are atypical and must not obscure the principal distinction between games and legal systems. In legal systems rules merely *regulate* activities, they do not constitute them. A judge administers a rule-regulated activity; an umpire judges a rule-constituted activity. The rules of law are followed and applied for reasons other than playing the law-game. The actions, decisions and activities which are governed by legal rules are not exclusively defined by them. To cite Max Black's example, one does not park a car in order to follow rules about parking. One would also park a car in a village which has no parking regulations at all.[8] The rules of a game on the other hand are applied and followed for the sake of playing the game. Cheating is to pretend that one is playing the game although one is secretly breaking the rules. When players cheat they do not 'really' play the game at all. In playing a game one cannot disobey or violate the rules. One can only cheat or make mistakes. The rules of a game, therefore, have a peculiarly strong binding force. All participating players necessarily follow the rules, for this is what is meant by playing a game. Where the players agree to change or modify the rules this is tantamount to stop playing that *version* of the game. Every player must necessarily follow the rules so long as he plays. Unlike legal rules, the rules of a game cannot be broken. This distinction between rule-constituted and rule-regulated activity is related to the distinction between open and closed orders, between *a priori* and empirical knowledge. Waismann comments that,

'Incompleteness, in the senses referred to, [in the discussion of open-texture] is the mark of empirical knowledge as opposed to *a priori* knowledge such as mathematics. In fact, it is the criterion by which we can distinguish perfectly *formalized* languages constructed by logicians from *natural* languages as used in describing reality. In a formalized system, the use of each symbol is governed by a definitive number of rules, and further, all the rules of inference and procedure can be stated completely. In view of the incompleteness which permeates empirical knowledge such a demand cannot be fulfilled by any language we may use to express it.'[9]

The demands of formalized systems cannot be fulfilled in reasoning with rules any more than in empirical knowledge. Disputes and conflicts of interests are a social fact, and courts are called upon to settle not only those aspects of disputes which are noticed in the *protasis* of legal rules. If courts were to disregard 'significant' factual distinctions, the cases they would then be deciding would bear little resemblance to the issues agitating the parties. Legal decisions are designed to settle issues arising out of actual situations which are themselves the product of complex and concurrent valuations. The reduction of the material facts of a case to *only* those facts which correspond to the *protasis* of existing rules of law, must, therefore, contradict the very function and rationality of the institution of adjudication; just as consideration of *every* fact of a case which agitates the parties would be incompatible with a system using rules. It is significant, for instance, that legal claims in contract can be defeated in contingencies of an essentially open-ended nature, such as duress or fraud. It was Hart who pointed out that no adequate characterization of the legal concept of a contract could be made without reference to the heterogeneous defences available in contractual actions, and the manner in which they serve to defeat or weaken contractual claims.[10]

In our example of the rescue in the park, it is evident that the rule excluding vehicles from the park cannot be relied upon to discriminate *by itself* between material and irrelevant facts. The rule mentions vehicles generally but it is silent about rescues. The rule will not tell whether the fact that rescue is involved requires that a distinction be made. As this example suggests there is indeed a considerable degree of interaction between rule and fact; we now examine the influence of rules on the selection of facts and we have already seen how the facts indicate which rule is applicable in the first place. There are situations, however, in which but for the legal rule some facts might go unnoticed. For example, in the case of a boy accused of theft, his date of birth is relevant, for the criminal law does not attribute criminal responsibility to the acts of children below a certain age. And this fact – his date of birth – is relevant even though no reference to it might have been made under a different penal system in which all children are held to be criminally responsible.

Systems of rules which regulate, rather than constitute, activities face, therefore, a difficulty which is not shared by *a priori* system in which activities are defined by the rules. Since the activities regulated are not so defined, other standards are needed to identify them. The application of rules in rule-regulated fields must then presuppose the application of additional standards of materiality for the selection of material facts. This means that the application of rules in such fields requires a determination of materiality which is partly dependent upon other systems of rules and standards. The expectation then that legal rules can be used to govern legal judgments to the exclusion of other rules is groundless. It now appears that non-legal standards are infused at a crucial step in the process of applying legal rules. This permits a generalization: the application of rules belonging to a system which regulates rather than constitutes activities, necessarily presupposes resort to concurrent standards of valuation as well, or to use a metaphor, the use of one tool for guiding inference often requires the use of allied tools, just as some jobs require the use of both hammers and screwdrivers.

Standards by which facts are relevant:
(ii) Maxims and rules of interpretation

In order to weed the wild garden of facts, it is necessary to utilize tables of significant facts for the identification of those facts that must not be rooted out. The use of one table covering a single species of such facts does not work, since it leads to discarding valuable specimens. More than one table is needed to cover all the species of facts which must be conserved. One such table is a table of the rules and maxims of interpretation, which direct the application of other rules. These rules and maxims point to circumstances which may be overlooked if reference were made to legal rules only. Thus the rule requiring that a statute be interpreted in the light of the purpose behind it, may require the consideration of facts relevant to the accomplishment of legislative policies. It thus calls for a consideration of 'facts' like the 'intention of Congress', the state of affairs that Congress desired to bring about. The facts to which such rules of interpretation draw attention are here referred to as 'interpretative facts'. They must be distinguished from those facts of a situation which are part of the datum of the issue or controversy to be decided. These interpretative facts influence the selection of the material facts, since testimony relevant to the purpose of a rule is unquestionably material. Consideration of such facts is essential for the proper application of rules even if their relevance to the applicable rule of law is not manifest. This can be illustrated by the remarkable case of *Smith v. Hiatt* decided in the Supreme Judicial Court of Massachusetts in 1952.[11]

This case involves the Massachusetts Public Ways and Works Statute which deals also with the repair of ways and bridges. The statute deals generally with the removal of snow and ice for the convenience of travellers. Section 21 of the statute in the chapter on the Repair of Ways and Bridges, refers to actions for injuries from snow and ice where such injuries are suffered on private property. The statute provides that notice of claims must be given in writing to the owners of the premises within a certain period of time. In this case an action for injuries was brought by Miss Smith, a nurse, who looked after the baby of Mrs Hiatt in Mrs Hiatt's home in Worcester. On a July morning, 'the plaintiff went to the kitchen to prepare milk for the baby. She there found Mrs Hiatt who had been defrosting the refrigerator. There was ice on the floor which Mrs Hiatt had dropped. . . . The plaintiff slipped on the ice and was injured'. Mrs Hiatt was present when the accident occurred.

The Supreme Judicial Court of Massachusetts held that the statute – which deals primarily with the removal of snow and ice from highways (and incidentally from private property) – applies to a case concerning the defrosting of a refrigerator in midsummer. The court ruled that under the statute the plaintiff was required to give notice of the claim in writing and that Miss Smith was not relieved from giving this notice by the fact that the owner was personally present at the scene of the accident.

What are the grounds for criticizing this judgment? The absurdity of the decision may be due to the Court's failure to take into consideration the facts which were relevant to the purpose of the statute. Clearly the statute was concerned with the clearing of snow and ice, and with giving notice of injuries arising from failure to remove snow and ice. It was concerned with the severe winter conditions that affect the Commonwealth of Massachusetts.

The Court, however, took a narrow view of the material facts: (1) that the injury was caused by ice (2) on the private property of the defendant (3) and that no notice of the claim had been given in writing. The Court ignored the fact that the accident had occurred in summer, not as the result of weather conditions but as the result of defrosting a refrigerator. It thus failed to take into account a facet of the case which had a direct bearing on the purpose of the statute: snow and ice clearance in New England winters. The judgment of the Court was, therefore, based on an incomplete view of the material facts. In the opinion of the Court, the material facts corresponded with the operative facts of the notice-for-injuries rule. But this correspondence ignored facts, which by virtue of the rule that a statute must be interpreted in the light of its purposes, ought also to have been considered. The Court used too narrow a criterion for selecting the material facts. The result was the reduced rationality of the decision.

Standards by which facts are relevant:
(iii) Moral rules and principles

There are other criteria as well. A court cannot be content to consider only those facts which are relevant to legal rules or to the rules of interpretation. By ignoring facts relevant to moral rules and principles, a court would cut itself off from much of the total setting of a case, with the detrimental effects already noticed in trials by chance. A rational decision – and this requires repetition – must be a decision of the *total situation* in which it occurs. Facts, which have moral or ethical significance, form part of this 'total situation'.

Morally significant facts often correspond to the *protasis* of moral rules. They form part of the circumstances indicated as material by moral rules and principles. They form part of the situation in which legal rules are applied. Every man, as a member of the community, shares at least some moral principles and values with other members. This sense of values is expressed in everything that is noticed and talked about – in every account, testimony and description. In issues of liability, for example, matters of intention are generally considered relevant, though the law, for reasons of public policy, may rule otherwise. Without a knowledge of the attitudes, values and meanings attached to occurrences, the occurrences themselves may become incomprehensible and meaningless. Just as the advance of ethics is a function of the recognition of the significance of conduct in its total setting, so the development of criminal law and of the law of torts is a function of the recognition of more refined factual distinctions.

In the case of our overworked example of the rescue in the park, parts of the testimony are pertinent to general standards of morality. The fact that I drove into the park with the intent to assist an injured person, and the fact that I was drunk and drove through a playground at great speed are both 'morally' relevant, and might well be considered by the court in the attribution of guilt or in the sentence. The intention, degree of care, and the state of mind of the accused are fundamental considerations in our moral thinking which have marked the law.

In most litigation, the relevance of facts which have ethical significance is so 'obvious' that it is hardly noticed at all. Such facts are concealed from our attention by the protective colouring of the obvious. Wittgenstein remarked that,

'The aspects of things that are most important for us are hidden because of their simplicity and familiarity. (One is unable to notice something because it is always before one's eyes.) The real foundations of his inquiry do not strike a man at all. Unless *that* fact has at some time struck him. – And this means: we fail to be struck by what, once seen, is most striking and most powerful.'[12]

This can be illustrated by the Central Park elephant murder case. In this case Z was arrested for intentionally shooting and killing an elephant in the park zoo, because of grievances against the management of the zoo arising from his dismissal as elephant keeper. In the trial, the examination of the witnesses brought out a variety of facts. Two facts, however, were never mentioned: the colour of Z's clothes on the day of the shooting and the colour of the elephant's skin. There was nothing unusual in this, for both these facts were quite obviously immaterial. This case must be contrasted with another case that occurred in Burma. All the circumstances, the nature of the offence, the motives of the accused, were in all respects identical to those which surrounded the Central Park case. The only difference between the two cases was that one arose in the U.S. and the other in Burma. There too, a variety of facts was brought to the attention of the court but for the same two facts: the colour of the clothes of the accused and the colour of the elephant's skin. In both instances, however, the elephant was a white elephant. The colour of the elephant was of no special interest in the U.S. (except perhaps in connection with its value) but it was of crucial importance in Burma, where white elephants are sacred and their slaughter sacrilegious. To omit in Burma any reference to the colour of the elephant was tantamount to concealing from the court a most important fact.

Facts and cows have this in common: they may be sacred in India but not in the U.S. The importance of cows and the relevance of what happens to them depends on their place and function in the community; what may be significant here may be – to enrich our metaphor – a red herring elsewhere.

Standards by which facts are relevant:
(iv) Economic and social considerations

The economic and social purposes of legal rules are in a sense merely particular aspects of their general purposes. When a statute has an economic purpose as an object, only experts may be able to assess the consequences of economic measures and their bearing on the overall policy of legislation. Economists and lawyers are then called upon to work together, and to agree on the significant and relevant features of the case. The nature of this collaboration is illuminating,

'[The lawyer] has to determine what matters of economic fact the existing formulations of legal doctrine make relevant, as well as how these matters are to be proved. If the law is unsettled and growing and the problem has novel elements, he must also consider what matters of economic fact a court or administrative agency may judge to be relevant. . . . the economist is the expert in observing economic behaviour and appraising economic effects, and he must have some degree of freedom in making his observations and appraisal. Again and again he will notice economic phenomena which the lawyer would miss but which, when called to the lawyer's attention, will seem to alter the character of the legal problem. So the truth is that neither [the lawyer nor the economist] can be in complete command.'[13]

In such situations the facts relevant to the economic purposes of the law 'may alter the character of the legal problem'. The distinguishing feature of these facts is the expertise required to discover them – an expertise of a scientific character – which seeks to establish the causal rather than the legal link between various acts and policies.

Standards by which facts are relevant:
(v) Consequences of proposed decisions

Rules and other inference devices presuppose some end-in-view. There is something odd about a gratuitous rule: a sign in a pond which reads 'do not attach boats to this sign'. Dewey perceptively stressed the significance of consequences in the application of laws. Clearly, the application of a rule giving rise to consequences incompatible with its end-in-view is defective in some respect. An assessment of the consequences of such application demands that all facts having a bearing on the consequences be fully canvassed. In *Gideon's* case, for example, the Supreme Court of the United States was concerned also with facts other than those surrounding the personal circumstances of the prisoner, Clarence Gideon.[14] In oral argument, the Court questioned the effect of granting the appeal in terms of the release of other prisoners in Gideon's position. It was concerned that its decision could lead to the sudden release of thousands of dangerous criminals thereby defeating one of the purposes of the criminal law. The situation, number and records of prisoners convicted without the benefit of counsel thus became a fact material to the decision of the case. The court clearly wished to be informed of the causal connection between the situation confronting it and the consequences of the advocated decision. It is now customary to inform the Court of the social consequences of its rulings, and the so-called Brandeis brief indicates the scope of the facts which the Court estimates to have a bearing on its judgments. Significantly, such facts are generally independent of the circumstances surrounding the parties to litigation. Considerations of justice, charity and compassion on the other hand, may be dictated by the impact of decisions on the parties litigant themselves. Facts pointing to harsh and unusual consequences of court action are thus equally material to the application of rules, for 'justice', whatever it may be, is certainly still one of the goals of the administration of justice.

Standards by which facts are material in other contexts

In the social sciences it is now generally recognized that 'facts' are not objective – there to be verified – datum just waiting to be noticed and considered. The material facts for the purposes of research in the social sciences are tainted by value and bias. The following citations are explicit,

'. . . our values and rules determine the manner in which we approach, see, arrange, and interpret, the facts.'[15]

'There is no other device for excluding biases in the social sciences than to face the valuations and to introduce them as explicitly stated, specific, and sufficiently concretized, value premises. If this is done, it will be possible to determine in a rational way, and openly to account for, the direction of theoretical research. It will further be possible to cleanse the scientific workshop from concealed, but ever resurgent, distorting valuations. Practical conclusions may thus be reached by rational inferences from the data and the value premises. Only in this way does social engineering, as an advanced branch of social research, become a rational discipline under full scientific control.'[16]

In the social sciences concerned with description, prediction and control, the seepage of value is regrettable. The social scientist seeks to prevent the excessive value-contamination of his facts – if he cannot do so, he should at least try to expose the values and biases underlying his work. The natural sciences possess an implicit standard of relevance, which, as we have already seen, is freer from the vagaries of human volition and preferences. This is the standard of empirical verification; whatever may affect prediction and control, is worthy of verification. But scientists like Polanyi testify that even in the natural sciences, bias and value play a considerable role in the selection and determination of material factors.[17] Moreover, in the social sciences, empirical verification cannot always be readily resorted to: it is impossible to conduct experiments isolating separate elements. There is the added difficulty encountered also in Quantum physics – that observation itself affects the conduct of the thing observed. It is reported, for example, that Navaho Indians have been selling anthropological information to eager doctoral students.

In speaking of relevance, a basic distinction between the method of the sciences and the method of rule-guided reasoning must, therefore, be kept in mind. While it is the purpose of the sciences to keep facts as value-free as possible, it is of the essence of the normative fields to seek the correspondence between facts, rules and their purposes. In the normative fields it must be recognized that the total situation of a case is man-selected, that it is the outcome of human valuation, and moreover that it is with human rules and purposes that the decision must be reached. Neither legal nor moral reasoning can afford to treat the intrusion of the human element as regrettable, either in the detection of the material facts or in the method of settling controversies. In the social sciences, the sensible attitude towards value is one of guarded hostility, and the intrusion of value may be inevitable. In the decisional fields it is essential – it is part of the logic of reasoning with rules.

In this chapter we have looked at material facts principally in the context of legal argument – but these observations apply to moral decisions as well. In ethics, the selection of material facts is no less important than in law, but since there are no authoritative collections of moral rules and principles, the problem of correspondence between material facts and moral rules has always remained rather blurred. All that a moral code can then require, is that judgment be based upon the fullest possible view of the total situation. The vagueness and looseness of moral deliberation, the absence of moral courts, and of established procedures of moral reasoning have all contributed to conceal the issue of the selection of material facts. In moral as in legal decision, the criteria which must be taken into account for the selection of the material facts are numerous, and it might be necessary to consider not only moral rules and principles but also legal rules and the social, economic and human purposes behind the rules. The situation is thus very similar to that prevailing in adjudication.

To recapitulate, the selection of the material facts of a case is fashioned by a variety of considerations. These cannot be neatly catalogued and listed. We have attempted to identify the more persistent and recurring standards by which facts are chosen as material:

  i. the applicable rule of law,
 ii. interpretative facts,
iii. moral rules and principles,
 iv. economic and social purposes,
  v. consequences of advocated decisions.

These standards operate concurrently and we use them without normally articulating them. There is nothing more surprising in this than in being able to speak English correctly without being able to spell out the rules of grammar observed. This concurrent operation may be illustrated by an analogy: there is a mutual pull between the earth and the moon. This mutual pull does not account for all the earth's movements. Other heavenly bodies such as the sun and the planets also affect them. It is impossible to give any *one* explanation for the movement and rotation of the earth. Even if the influence of the sun is the single most important factor, others such as variations in the earth's magnetic field, may account for slight changes in the speed of the rotation of the earth on its axis. A full account of the influences that matter would, therefore, include a variety of factors. Similarly the 'full setting' of a situation which requires a decision, is the outcome of the concurrent operation of a variety of standards. To the extent that we refine our knowledge of the 'full setting' of a situation, we can improve our decisions; just as by refining our knowledge of the influences which control the earth's motion we improve our predictions. Our determination of the 'facts' may be quite crude and imprecise, but in seeking improvement we also move towards better decisions.

E

REASONING WITH RULES:
SOME OTHER NECESSARY INGREDIENTS

It is a commonplace that a legal decision involves two elements: legal rules and the facts of the case. This commonplace suppresses, however, other aspects of reasoning with rules:

  i. the *process* of reasoning from facts to decision;
  ii. the statement of the inference drawn;
  iii. the statement of the governing rule – when an opinion is rendered – which must not be confused with preexisting formulations of the rule;
  iv. the decision or verdict;
  v. the foreseeable consequences of the decision;
  vi. the foreseeable applicability of the statement of the governing rule. Let us take these in turn.

The process of reasoning from facts to decision

Gilbert Ryle said that 'Investigations are not the only occupations in which we apply our minds'.[1] When we follow or apply a rule we also apply our minds. Such an occupation is a 'clockable occurrence'.[2] We apply our minds when 'we look to the rule for instruction and *do something*, without appealing to anything else for guidance'.[3] The nature of what it is that rules guide is clarified by the following passage from Wittgenstein's *Philosophical Investigations*,

'Let us consider the experience of being guided, and ask ourselves: what does this experience consist in when for instance our *course* is guided? – Imagine the following cases:
You are in a playing field with your eyes bandaged, and someone leads you by the hand, sometimes left, sometimes right; you have constantly to be ready for the tug of his hand, and must also take care not to stumble when he gives an unexpected tug.
Or again: someone leads you by the hand where you are unwilling to go, by force.
Or: you are guided by a partner in a dance; you make yourself as

receptive as possible, in order to guess his intention and obey the slightest pressure. . . .'[4]

Evidently, rules do not guide *physical* movements. To use a metaphor, they are more like the letters of the alphabet which enable us to read. When we let ourselves be guided by letters,

'We imagine that a feeling enables us to perceive as it were a connecting mechanism between the look of the word and the sound that we utter. For when I speak of the experiences of being influenced, [by letters] of causal connexion, of being guided, that is really meant to imply that I as it were feel the movement of the lever which connects seeing the letters with speaking.'[5]

When we use a rule we allow our minds to be guided just as when we dance we let our steps and bodies be guided. We may not always understand what a mental process is, but surely we are familiar with what it is to let our reasoning be guided. We can ask what it was, what took place when we suddenly reached a conclusion.[6] When we allow our reasoning to be guided by a rule, we feel that the rule is the reason why we concluded such and such; we then justify the reasoning by the rule.[7]

To follow or to apply a rule involves then a mental occurrence which must not be misrepresented as a mere matter of 'feeling' in contrast to verifiable physical phenomena.[8] The mental occurrences involved in reasoning with rules cannot be verified by observations since they refer to operations of the mind. We can at best have circumstantial evidence for them. For example, when someone says that he is reading, it is impossible to tell by merely observing him whether he is really reading or merely holding the book and running his eyes. The best evidence that we can expect to get is by questioning him about the text. And this is not very reliable evidence; he may have been told, or he may have read it a long time ago. But surely even though we cannot verify directly whether he is reading or merely pretending to, we are not prepared to dismiss the activity of reading as metaphysical or to consider it as an emotive process.[9] What matters here is that the process of reasoning guided by a rule is a mental activity distinct from the rule guiding it and the context in which it is applied.

Waismann reached a related conclusion in the field of natural science: the relationship between laws and their application is of a looser character than it has generally been thought.[10] He noted that no observational statements can be logically connected with the premises of any laws, that the relations of logic can only hold between statements which belong to a 'homogeneous domain' and that the deductive nexus can never extend beyond the limits of such a domain. The step from laws to their application, therefore, involves an inevitable logical type-jump – the jump from what Ryle calls 'law-statements' to 'episodic statements'. And this jump involves the *doing* of something, albeit something mental. The relation between laws of any kind and the occurrences to which they relate is one of correspondence rather than formal logic. There is no strict logical relation between law and facts; and there can never be any. This relationship cannot be a logical one in the analytic sense for it is the relationship between two strata of language, between two languages so to speak. A correspondence between two strata of language – the language of laws and the language of occurrences – is the characteristic mark of working logic, of logic in use. Interpretation is the *process of establishing* this correspondence, of moving from one stratum to the other. It functions where formal logic is silent; it connects concepts in logically heterogeneous domains.

In the application of legal rules, it is often very easy to overlook the *process* of reasoning especially where the inference is so obvious that it is hardly noticeable. As Mr Justice Cardozo observed,

'Of the cases that come before the court in which I sit, a majority, I think, could not, with semblance of reason, be decided in any way but one. The law and its application alike are plain. Such cases are predestined, so to speak, to affirmance without opinion.'[11]

However, even in the plainest case, a mental operation is involved which connects the rule, the facts and the decision. It is a psychological phenomenon that in obvious cases rules are applied quasi-automatically, with practically no heed and that there is a feeling the decision is 'predestined'. Nevertheless, even in these cases, a linking must take place, leading from the facts to the conclusion or decision of the court. The linking is accompanied by a certain experience of transition from facts to conclusions.

The inferring from facts to conclusions necessarily involves the selection of some facts as material. This we have already pointed out. But we are now perhaps in a better position to appreciate what is involved in such inferring. To take an example, a person who learns the arabic script may have difficulties in distinguishing the characters of the script from other flourishes and marks. An experienced reader on the other hand would have no trouble telling letters from other signs, and would easily identify merely decorative arabesques. Similarly, inferring necessarily involves proceeding from some facts to conclusions. It is a process which presupposes the related process of identifying the facts that matter. This process of *singling* out material facts is necessarily involved in *proceeding* from facts to conclusions.[12] Whether this is one composite or two related processes matters little. This sequence of mental operations must not be equated with mere feelings and states of minds. It involves the use of a mental faculty. There is a danger of confusing states of mind and mental processes.

Statement of the inference drawn

Opinions of courts are *evidence* of mental processes. Opinions generally contain statements of preexisting rules of law as well as formulations of the inferences drawn. These formulations are distinct from the actual inferring and yet do not purport to describe the process of reasoning. A descriptive account of such a mental process would include psychological datum and other information about the person of the judge.[13] The formulation of an inference drawn is not intended to impart information about a judge. It is designed to state the inference which the judge considered the rule to require. In reading an opinion it is easy to confuse the logical status of the ingredients of which it is made up. This can be illustrated by the familiar example of the vehicle in the park. The park regulation does not say what happened in my case. It is silent about particular events. The statement of the facts, the park regulation and the order of the court do not constitute a satisfactory account of the reasoning of the court:

'the accused drove into the park' (fact),
'no vehicles are allowed in the park' (rule),
'the accused is guilty' (decision).

These three statements are not connected until a *process* of reasoning creates a link between them. It would be like claiming that the following three statements amount to a report that someone made a journey from New York to Boston:

'Harry went to New York, Grand Central station',
'A railway ticket from New York to Boston',
'Harry arrived at Boston railway station'.

It is easy to confuse the logical categories of a law-statement like, 'No vehicles are allowed in the park' with the formulation of an inference, 'Since the accused has driven a car into the park he is guilty of a breach of law'. The following three statements do include on the other hand an account of an inference:

'The accused drove into the park' (fact),

'Since the accused has driven into the park he is guilty of a breach of law' (statement of inference),

'The accused is guilty of a breach of the law prohibiting vehicles in the park' (decision).

The distinction between a statement of inference and the rule which warrants it can be stated in a more formal way:

'X did A' (fact),

'All who do X are guilty of B' (rule),

'Verdict: X is guilty of B' (decision).

Contrast this with:

'X did A' (fact),

'All who do X are guilty of B' (rule),

'Since X did A he is guilty of B' (statement of inference),

'Verdict: X is guilty of B' (decision).

The distinction between the two sets of statements is important. The first set is a sequence of statements which require a connection. The conclusion of the first set of statements does not necessarily follow from the two premises. A substantial step, an inference, is required to reach the conclusion. In the second set, on the other hand, the conclusion is only a rearrangement of the terms contained in the first three statements.

Let us take another example. This one involves driving a tricycle without a licence. There is a rule providing: 'No locomotives may be driven without a licence.' The question is whether for the purposes of the rule a tricycle is a locomotive. This rather odd example is suggested by an English case under the 1865 Locomotives Act, *Parkyns v. Preist*[14] in which it was held that tricycles propelled by steam were locomotives under the Act. This incidentally perhaps explains why the holder of an ordinary English driving licence is entitled to drive a 'heavy locomotive, light locomotive . . . or motor tricycle equipped with means for reversing . . .'. In such a case the problem of interpretation is to determine the scope of the inference warranted by the legal rule.

It is possible to state every legal inference in traditional syllogistic form, i.e., so that the decision of the court is simply a formal transformation of the premises on which it relies. It is thus possible to make two syllogistic arguments which contradict each other, and which are nevertheless, true:

'All who do A are guilty of B',

'X did A',

'So X is guilty of B'; and:

'All who do C are not guilty of B',

'X did C',

'So X is not guilty of B'.

Each of the two sets of arguments is a syllogism, and a court may be faced with parallel or competing sets of syllogistic arguments. To say then that an argument is syllogistic is no particular help. So that the question arises whether the syllogistic form of arguments is of any significance or whether it is only a logician's device for classifying them. Toulmin pointed out, in *The Uses of Argument* that some syllogistic arguments are not formally valid since they involve more than a strict transformation of their premises – that is, they 'say something'. Some syllogisms require a sub-stantial step, an inference, to move from the premises to the conclusion. This is significantly so in rule-guided reasoning. For, as we have seen the use of an inference-warrant or rule as a middle term does not inevitably lead to the conclusion, and a sub-stantial step of reasoning remains necessary.

We have thus added some refinement to the assertion that the correspondence between fact and rule is essential to rational decision-making. For this correspondence is not analytic but arises through the process of reasoning (inference), which is based on the material facts on one hand and which is warranted by the legal rule on the other.

The enunciation of the rule justifying the decision; rules of guidance and rules of justification

Drawing distinctions may become an addiction for the philo-sophically inclined. Self-indulgence in this respect can clutter up thought with drifting remnants of pointless distinctions. Yet, despite this threat, more distinctions are here in order, and failure to draw them can only result in confused theories about the use of rules.

It has already been observed that rules lend themselves to re-formulation. Both Wittgenstein and Max Black recognized this.[15] This feature plays an important role in the use of precedents and example. We have characterized rules as inference-guidance devices leading to choice, decision and judgment. Inference-guidance devices are obviously designed for use in cases subsequent to their promulgation; in other words, to follow a rule evidently involves a preexisting rule. In delivering opinions courts are not generally content to refer to such preexisting rules and there to let the matter rest. They do something more, and they often *enunciate* the rule governing the case before them by reformulating the preexisting rule. A New York case discussed by Llewellyn provides a good example of this technique:

Technically speaking there is a marked distinction between issuing a draft, or traveller's cheque and receiving money for transmission (preexisting rule).	Technically speaking there is a marked distinction between issuing a draft, or traveller's cheque *or transferring money by cable* and receiving money for *actual* transmission (reformulated rule; passages in italics were added in reformulation).[16]

In adding these words the Court did nothing dishonest. It believed that the reformulation was warranted by the preexisting statement of the rule. It was merely 'standing' on a point. It believed that the preexisting rule did not only warrant the drawing of the inference but that it also authorized the reformulation of the governing principle. This reformulation is distinct in one vital respect from the preexisting rule which authorized it. It is not, and obviously cannot be, an inference-guidance device for the decision of *that* case. *It is a rule of justification rather than a rule of guidance.*

This difference must now be explored. Let us take an example: *McBoyle v. U.S.* involved the construction of the National Motor Vehicle Theft Act of 1919.[17] The question before the Supreme Court of the U.S. was whether the Act applied to aircraft. The petitioner had been convicted of transporting from Illinois to Oklahoma an airplane which he knew to have been stolen. The Act defined 'motor vehicle' to include 'automobile, automobile truck, automobile wagon, motor cycle, or any other self-propelled vehicle not designed for running on rails.' The preexisting rule thus made the theft of 'any other self-propelled vehicle not designed for running on rails' punishable under the Act. Mr Justice Holmes reformulated this preexisting rule so as to exclude aircrafts '. . . it is impossible to read words that so carefully enumerate the different forms of motor vehicles and have no reference of any kind to aircraft, as including airplanes under a term that usage more and more precisely confines to a different class.' The reformulated rule thus made the theft of any self-propelled vehicle not designed for running on rails, but excluding aircraft, punishable under the Act. This is an instance of 'interpretation' as Wittgenstein would have us use the word,

'. . . there is an inclination to say: every action according to the rule is an interpretation. But we ought to restrict the term "interpretation" to the substitution of one expression of the rule for another.'[18]

In the *McBoyle* case the substitution of the rule excluding aircraft does not perform the same role which the rule it is replacing had performed. The original statutory definition of 'vehicle' was designed as an inference-guidance device guiding the reasoning of the courts, but the substituted definition merely justified the holding of the Supreme Court; it did not guide it. This does not mean that it cannot be used in subsequent cases as an inference-guidance device, but this is another matter. There is something peculiar about the way in which a rule of justification operates. Although it does not function as an inference-guidance device for the court which enunciates it, it is nevertheless designed to guide the ratiocination of those who may desire to examine the decision, among whom the other members of the bench figure prominently. It is designed to help such persons reach the very same decision and make the very same inference. It is formulated, in other words, with a view to checking or *going over* the decision and the inference. It must, however, itself be authorized by the preexisting rule. It must also be *necessary* to explain the holding which it justifies.

In many cases there is no need for the enunciation of a rule of justification. The preexisting rule suffices, for its application is then obvious. But where the application of such preexisting rule leaves some doubt, when it is not manifest that the inference made is warranted, then a statement of justification would guide the person going over the decision more firmly than the preexisting rule could. Such a statement makes the inference easier and more direct. It provides so to speak a detailed map where only a general map was available before.

Statements offered as justification are, however, amenable to criticism when it can be shown that they were not authorized by a preexisting rule, and that a court, therefore, must have stated the law wrongly. They can also be criticized if they are not necessary for the justification of a decision or if they are broader than required.

The role of a statement enunciated by a court in the process of deciding a case does not terminate with the conclusion of the case. Such a statement is a normative statement of the most promising manufacture: fashioned in the glare of adversary argument, under the ever present power of superior courts to overrule or limit, in the anvil of concrete sets of material facts and with the hammer of existing rules. Such statements do not, therefore, merely justify the decisions of the cases in which they are first enunciated. It should be possible to use them in subsequent cases as inference-guidance devices of the same weight as the inference-guidance device which authorized them in the first place. This shall be examined in the next section.

The decision, its consequences and the scope of the statement enunciated

These additional elements must also briefly be identified. The decisions, verdicts or orders of a court contain the formal disposition of a case. They generally consist of specific instructions addressed to the parties; to another court or to some state organ. They are that part of a decision which most closely interests the parties. They furnish the basis of enforcement action in civil cases and this is where the connection between civil law and state enforcement is the closest. In criminal matters two separate steps are generally involved in the disposition of a case: the verdict of guilty (or not guilty) and the sentencing. Sentencing is often a matter left to the determination of the judges within broad statutory guidelines. It involves considerations wholly different from those taken into account for the establishment of guilt. Sentencing is not ordinarily dictated by rules which stipulate punishment. We here refer to the formal disposition of a case by way of an order or verdict as 'the decision'.

Every decision necessarily leads to some reasonably foreseeable consequences for the parties and for those closely associated with them. These may at times be diametrically opposed to the purposes of the rule which governs the decision, or conflict with the interests and policies normally upheld by the rules of the legal system. Harsh results may require modification of the rule applied. This is suggested by the dictum that hard cases make bad law. Courts must thus consider the contemplated consequences of decisions and their compatibility with the rules, the interests and final commitments which they generally uphold. This element in rational deliberation has been much stressed by the pragmatists and notably by Dewey in his analysis of the logic of judgments of practice.[19] Its disregard would certainly be irrational, for it would allow decisions to become self-contradicting and destructive of the very policies and interests which the rules seek to uphold.

Although the consequences of a decision are innumerable, just as the facts of a case to be decided, they are not all 'material'. It is thus again necessary to identify the criterion in terms of which the material consequences can be distinguished from those that are irrelevant. We shall see that the purposes of the rule applied and those of other rules upheld by the legal system furnish the standards in terms of which it is possible to evaluate these consequences. The foreseeable consequences of a decision for the parties involved and for those associated with them are here referred to as the 'consequences of the decision'.

We have already examined the concern of the Supreme Court in *Gideon's* case with foreseeable consequences.[20] That case involved the question whether the Supreme Court's decision in the case of *Betts v. Brady* should be overruled and whether the right to counsel was so fundamental that the Due Process clause of the Fourteenth Amendment required the provision of a lawyer in all state cases for those too poor to retain their own. As we have already indicated, argument in the case was directed to the consequences of the universal counsel requirement on the continued imprisonment of prisoners already convicted without the benefit of counsel. The Court was thus warned by the State of Florida that one consequence of adopting the universal counsel requirement would be to render eligible for release 5,093 hardened criminals out of the 7,836 inmates of the Florida State prisons, not to mention other prisoners similarly placed in other states. Another aspect of the Court's questioning touched upon Federal intervention in state criminal proceedings, and the point was made that the Court's decision in *Betts v. Brady* had meant more, not less, Federal intervention. Now these two considerations were clearly material to the Court's decision. The Court was certainly sensitive to the argument that its decision might have the effect of threatening the public safety by causing the release of dangerous criminals from jail, and it was also sensitive to the suggestion that its previous decision in the *Betts* case had led to much interference with the criminal proceedings of the several states. The Court sought both to uphold the public safety and to prevent Federal intervention whenever possible; these were considerations that it had to take into account. These considerations are not properly speaking consequences at all. What was really involved was something else. The Supreme Court was debating with counsel the scope of inferences which the advocated ruling would require and it was debating the probable implications of the decisions that would be warranted by these inferences.[22] The distinction we are here aiming at is between a consideration of the consequences of an order or 'decision' and those of enunciating a particular rule or principle. The first set of consequences involves only the parties to the dispute, the second involves the prospective use and scope of application of the rule formulated.

The contemplated applications of the rule advocated play a considerable role in shaping it. To take an example, Professor Wechsler has criticized the Supreme Court decision of *Shelley v. Kraemer* on the ground that the principle it had enunciated in that case could not possibly be followed in subsequent cases without leading to impossible results.[23] He raised a general issue quite separate from that whether the Court could in fact follow in other situations its ruling that the enforcement of a restrictive covenant against the sale of a property to a Negro involved state action denying him equal protection. He challenged the holding that a state denies equal protection of the laws when its courts give effect to private discriminations on the ground that the Court could not have meant it as a principle of general applicability since courts every day give effect to private racial or religious discrimination in wills and the laws of trespass to private property. He argued that if the Court is not prepared to apply its principle to other cases involving private discrimination then it is no principle at all. What Professor Wechsler emphasized is that the Court must consider the impact of the rule enunciated on other cases and that such rule must have some area of general applicability. It is one thing, he argued, to anticipate future cases that perhaps may be distinguishable without now deciding the sufficiency of the distinction, and it is another to judge the present case in terms of a rule that is quite plainly unacceptable in the light of other cases that would be governed by it.[24] In effect, his criticism of *Shelley v. Kraemer* amounts to the demand that enunciated rules be usable as inference-warrants in subsequent decisions. The consideration of the foreseeable consequences of an enunciated rule should disclose the possibility of relying upon it in the future. It need not, however, in Professor Levi's words, 'steer a safe course for future conflicts'.[25] Although the role assigned to the Supreme Court of the United States to lay guidelines for the future may be somewhat unique, surely the logic of Professor Wechsler's criticism is the same in all cases in which rules or principles are enunciated without regard to the consequences of such enunciation. We would agree with Professor Henkin that,

'Philosophically, the thesis remains valid: the Court cannot properly decide a case on the basis of a "principle" that is not a principle because it is not intended and expected to apply generally to similar cases.'[26]

It would seem, in conclusion, that every legal decision is an amalgam not of two logical elements – facts and law – but of a variety of distinct ingredients which are not limited to legal reasoning but are common to various species of reasoning guided by rules:
  i. the facts on record;
  ii. the preexisting rule or precedent;
  iii. the process of (i) selecting the material facts and (ii) reasoning from the material facts to the required or desired conclusion;
  iv. the statement of the reasoning – or inference – drawn;
  v. the enunciation of the rule justifying the inference drawn (must not be confused with the preexisting rule);
  vi. the decision, order or verdict disposing of the case;
  vii. the foreseeable consequences of the decision;
  viii. the foreseeable application of the rule enunciated and its consequences.

We shall see in later chapters that this inventory of ingredients is not yet complete. It suffices, however, for an initial look at the doctrine of precedent and for an analysis of the differences between reasoning with rules and reasoning from examples.

PRECEDENT

Some concepts of precedent

The controversies over the use of precedent in common law countries are intimately connected with the logic of reasoning with rules. The principal questions here dealt with are (i) what is it in a precedent case that is binding on a later court? (ii) whose determination of the binding ingredient is decisive, the precedent court's or the deciding court's?

The theory of precedent involves three related concepts: the rule of *stare decisis et non quieta movere* which translated means 'to adhere to the decided and not unsettle the established'; the ambiguous concept of *ratio decidendi* which can be translated either as 'reason for deciding' or 'reason for decision' and its complement *obiter dictum* which literally means 'saying by the way'. At common law it is the *ratio decidendi* of a case that is binding in later cases and which is the keystone of the doctrine of *stare decisis*. Hence the importance of determining precisely the demarcation line between what, in a precedent case, is the *ratio* and what is *obiter*; this is a problem of less immediacy in legal systems like the French in which single decided cases are not binding authorities for later cases. The concern of the common law for distilling the concept of *ratio decidendi* furnishes an invaluable setting for the analysis of the nature of both the reason for deciding a case and of the reasoning in the decision of a case.[1]

English and American scholars now agree that the practice of courts with regard to the use of the concept of *ratio decidendi* is both unprincipled and inconsistent. As a matter of fact, courts in common law jurisdictions have been observed to equate 'precedent' with any reason which influences their ultimate decision, whether it be a finding of fact, a determination of law, an opinion about the policy of the law, or a principle of law which though manifestly *obiter* is relied upon to support a decision.[1] Thus Llewellyn lists in the *Common Law Tradition*, no less than sixty-four techniques for handling precedent.[2]

But court practices aside, there have been a number of scholarly debates on the nature of precedent which have received a measure of judicial recognition. In the first place scholars have discussed the so-called 'English theory' of precedent. It has been subjected to the criticism of Goodhart and Stone in an intricate web of articles, rejoinders and counter-rejoinders.[3] It has been described as the,

'... theory of precedent, [which] as formulated by text-writers, imports that a particular decision is explained by one *ratio decidendi*, or general proposition of which the particular decision is an application, and which is "required" or "necessary" to explain that particular decision.'[4]

In a 1930 article, Goodhart distinguished between the facts on the record and the facts noticed by the judge in his decision.[5] In Goodhart's view, the distinction between the facts which the judge in his opinion regards as material and those which he considers immaterial is the touchstone of the doctrine of *stare decisis*. For, in his view, the *ratio* of a case is not found in the reasons given by a judge, nor in the rule of law set forth in that opinion, but in taking account (a) of the facts treated by the judge as material and (b) his decision as based on them. The nature of this distinction is logical, but is neither descriptive nor prescriptive, and does not fit into the conventional dual mode of analysis outlined by Stone,

'one approach is that of the observer who seeks to describe and explain *as a matter of fact* how present decisions are related to prior decisions. The other approach seeks to establish from the behaviour of courts themselves, perhaps supplemented by assumed first principles, the limits within which, *as a matter of law*, a prior decision prescribes binding rules for later decisions.'[6]

Goodhart's analysis obviously eludes classification in these terms.

In a recent restatement of his position, Goodhart reaffirms the distinction between the rule propounded by a judge and the *ratio decidendi* of a case,

'The whole point of my article was based on the proposition that every case must contain a binding principle, but that this binding principle is not necessarily to be found in the statement of the law made by the judge.

'[Yet], [T]he reasons given by the judge in his opinion, or his statement of the rule of law which he is following, are of peculiar importance, for they furnish us with a guide for determining which facts he considered material and which immaterial.'[7]

Both Stone and Simpson stress the difficulty involved in the notion of material facts which is the touchstone of the Goodhart thesis. They both question the idea that facts exist only on one level of generality and suggest that the core of the difficulty in interpretation lies in choosing the proper level of generality of the material facts. Stone cites the well-known English case of *Donoghue v. Stevenson* as an example. This is the celebrated torts case of the snail in the ginger beer bottle, which is the basis of much of the modern English law of negligence. Stone asks which is the right level of generality of the material facts in this case?

'Dead snails *or* any snails, *or* any noxious physical foreign body, *or* any noxious foreign element, physical or not, *or* any noxious element; . . . An opaque bottle of ginger beer, *or* an opaque bottle of beverage, *or* any bottle of beverage, *or* any container of commodities for human consumption, *or* any containers or any chattels for human use, *or* any chattel whatsoever, *or* any thing (including land or buildings) . . .'[8]

The difficulty of the level of generality of the material facts arises, however, not in connection with drawing an inference, with reasoning in that case, but in connection with the use of the precedent as a warrant for subsequent inferences. It arises in interpreting a *ratio*.

Goodhart, in his theory of precedents, seems to be concerned only with the binding part of the decision. But where no precedent is directly binding, the distinction between the actual reasoning and the law statement expounded by the judge loses much of its significance. For then, the inference drawn on the material facts and the law statement enunciated both have persuasive authority only. As soon as it is realized that there is no strictly binding authority, the law statement gains importance. When the case to be decided slips from under the grip of a binding *ratio decidendi* the judge's leeway of choice is increased. Precedents supply tools of inference of varying binding power. They mostly contain both a strict *ratio*, an inference on the material facts, which is binding in later cases, and a statement of reasons which has persuasive authority in other cases. Montrose's critique of the Goodhart thesis is primarily based on the practice of courts.[9] Neither this critique nor any amount of court practice can, however, obliterate the logical distinctions between the inference and the reasons for the inference. But if Montrose is right, and the principles of law declared by judges in the course of judgment are the real stuff of precedent, there would remain little justification for making quite so sharp a distinction between *obiter dicta* and *rationes decidendi*. Montrose is, however, not quite right when he says that the practice of the courts conflicts with Goodhart's thesis. From Llewellyn's study, and from Goodhart's own examples, it seems that courts do treat both inferences and judges' formulations of their reasons as *rationes decidendi*.

Another theory, supported by Simpson, is characterized by Goodhart as the 'statement theory'. This is the theory that the judge's statement of the law in the case is the *ratio decidendi* of the case. Goodhart criticized it on two grounds, on the ground that every case must contain an ascertainable principle of law, even though no opinion may have been delivered by the judge, and on the ground that the statement may be too wide or too narrow.[10] In his defence of the statement theory, Simpson fails to distinguish between the judge's actual inference and the statement propounded in justification of the inference,

'Clearly it is very important to decide which is the *ratio*, but this decision is in no way assisted by any supposed distinction between rules on the one hand and statements of material facts plus conclusions on the other, for the latter is only a description [*sic*] of the former.'[11]

Simpson fails to recognize the significance of the distinction made by Goodhart. This is the distinction between a process – an inference from certain material facts to a certain conclusion – and between the enunciation of a rule justifying the inference. He is certainly wrong in saying that the one is only a description of the other. Simpson thus confuses the two questions: 'which rule did Lord Atkin conceive to be applicable in the case of *Donoghue v. Stevenson*?' and 'from which facts did the Court arrive at its decision?' He confuses the law statement enunciated by Lord Atkin with the inference drawn in accordance with it. Lord Atkin's rule – the neighbour principle – is merely Lord Atkin's formulation of what he believed the law to be; it is the justification for the inference he drew. Here is an excerpt from Atkin's speech which Goodhart would not regard as binding,

'In this way it can be ascertained at any time whether the law recognizes a duty, but only where the case can be referred to some particular species which has been examined and classified. And yet the duty which is common to all the cases where liability is established must logically be based upon some element common to the cases where it is found to exist. . . . There must be, and is, some general conception of relations giving rise to a duty of care, of which the particular cases found in the books are but instances.'[12]

The novel contribution of each case to the fabric of the law is *not* the judge's statement of what the law is. A judge's opinion as to what the law is does not always elicit the approval of his fellow judges; it is at best evidence concerning the existing legal rules, evidence whose weight varies with the esteem in which the judge is held. This is also the traditional view expressed by Blackstone,

'So that *the law*, and the *opinion of the judge*, are not always convertible terms, or one and the same thing; since it sometimes may happen that the judge may *mistake* the law. Upon the whole however, we may take it as a general rule, "that the decisions of courts of justice are the evidence of what is common law".'[13]

The unique element in every case is not the statement of the law made by the judge, but the inference drawn on the facts of the case. And it is this inference which, in the Goodhart theory, is transformed into a binding inference-warrant for subsequent cases.

Critique of some theories of ratio decidendi

Most contemporary theories on the nature of precedent can be restated in terms of the ingredients involved in reasoning with rules. This restatement facilitates the articulation of the necessary implications and consequences which they contain. Courts can rely on, or follow one or all of the following ingredients in a precedent case:
1. the 'inferring' in the precedent case from the material facts to the holding; this is a restatement of Goodhart's theory: 'I suggested that the principle of the case could be found by determining (a) the facts treated by the judge as material, and (b) his decision as based on them.';[14]
2. the rule enunciated in the precedent case; this is a restatement of Montrose's position: 'I have argued that it is better to use the phrase *ratio decidendi* to mean exclusively the principle of law propounded by the judge as the basis of his decision, a usage which would correspond with judicial usage.';[15]
3. the rule or principle which preexisted the precedent decision in which it was followed; this is a restatement of Salmond's position: 'the rule of law for which a case is of binding authority.'[16] It has

also been stated by Stone as the theory which imports that, 'a particular decision is explained by one *ratio decidendi*, or a general proposition of which the particular decision is an application.'[17]

Wasserstrom's 'three possible ways' of formulating a rule of decision of particular cases do not establish any other alternatives.[18] Indeed, it would seem hard to find in prior decisions other elements which could be used as inference-guidance devices unless one were willing to use mere obiters or naked policy considerations for this purpose.

(i) The inferring in the precedent case

Goodhart has repeatedly asserted that in analysing a case our task,

'. . . is not to state the facts and the conclusion, but to state the material facts as seen by the judge and his conclusion based on them. *It is by his choice of the material facts that the judge creates law.*'[19]

He wrote,

'I was careful to italicize the words I considered to be of particular importance. I then suggested various rules which would be of help in determining these material facts. Of these the most important is the rule that "the reasons given by the judge in his opinion, or his statement of the rule of law which he is following, are of peculiar importance, for they may furnish us with a guide for determining which facts he considered material and which immaterial".'[20]

In criticizing Goodhart's theory Stone argues that there are several alternative levels of statement for each material fact of a precedent case, ranging from the full unique concreteness of an actual case, through a series of widening generalizations.[21] He concludes that a later court cannot ascertain the 'correct' level of statement of each fact-element, and that, therefore, a material fact of a precedent case can be stated 'at various levels of generality, each of which is correct for that case'. Once this is granted, he argues that,

'. . . any of these levels of statement is potentially a "material fact". Insofar as the *ratio decidendi* is determined by each "material fact", then what the precedent case yields must be a number of potentially binding *rationes* competing *inter se* to govern future cases of which the facts may fall within one level of generality, but not within another.'[22]

It would seem, however, that Stone misconceives the nature of the 'inferring' in the precedent case. The 'inferring' refers to a *process* of reasoning on the facts chosen by the judge as material. These are the facts chosen *from* the record, in their full unique concreteness. If these facts include dead snails in a bottle of ginger-beer then it is from them that the judge makes his selection, and that is their level of generality. There is, in other words, only one inference actually drawn by the judge on the facts chosen by him as material. Admittedly when a court is constituted of more than one judge the matter is more complicated, but what matters is that every judge draws only one inference and no more. The level of generality of the material facts is a question which the judge would have to consider in formulating the *protasis* of the rule advanced in support of such inference, but it simply does not arise in connection with the process of inferring itself. The inferring proceeds from the facts chosen as material to the conclusion, it proceeds on the level of generality at which they are stated on the record. What confuses Stone, it would seem, is the role which these facts play in the later case. Quite obviously, the peculiar facts of a case are never likely exactly to recur. If this is so, Stone asks what possible use can they be for later cases since, as he argues,

'. . . a *ratio decidendi* drawn from a case by the "material facts" method can only be prescriptive or binding for a later case whose facts are "on all fours" *in every respect*. And since the italicized words must be taken seriously, this reduces the range of the binding *ratio decidendi* to vanishing point.'[23]

We respectfully disagree. When a *ratio* is drawn by the 'material facts' method, that is, when a court uses a precedent court's 'inferring' to guide its own inferring, it is bound to follow such reasoning *unless* it can establish that the facts in the case before it are *materially different* from those of the precedent case. It is up to the later court to distinguish a precedent it wants to avoid; it need not show that a precedent it wishes to follow is on all fours with the facts of the case it is deciding. Although this objection to Stone's criticism appears as a mere difference of emphasis, it lies in effect at the heart of the technique of reasoning with precedent.

Reasoning from case to case by the 'material facts' method involves a technique which is profoundly different from the technique of reasoning with rules: reasoning with examples requires the comparison of factual situations and the articulation of material differences between them if prior holdings are to be disregarded. Reasoning with examples, like reasoning with rules, is designed to ensure that similar cases are decided in the same way. It is, however, always up to the later court to show why it is not bound by what appears to be a case in point. When an 'inferring' – and we use this clumsy word in order to emphsize that we refer to the *process* of reasoning – warrants a later inferring, it then acts as an inference guidance device. It warrants the same holding unless the facts in the later case are shown to be materially different. If we consider then an 'inferring' as an inference-guidance device, the difficulty of the 'levels of generality of the material facts' disappears, and if we consider that it is up to the later court to articulate distinctions, we can avoid the problem of case law becoming a 'wilderness of single instances'.

Goodhart's position by no means implies that there are no standards for assessing such 'inferring'. We have already considered the factors that ought to be weighed in the selection of material facts, and quite obviously the reasoning from the facts chosen to the holding in the case must also be authorized or warranted by some preexisting rule of law, decision or principle. Both steps involved in the reasoning from facts to holding, are thus controlled by principle and law. Both are equally open to review in these terms.

(ii) The enunciated rule of the precedent case

This theory is also sometimes referred to as the 'classical theory'. It obviously requires that a distinction be drawn between the *dicta* and the *ratio* of a case. In writing an opinion, a judge can indulge in writing a treatise or attempt to codify the law. He can, if he wishes, enunciate legal principles of various levels of generality. As Levi pointed out,

'the particular view of a given judge on propositions of law can be decisive on future cases and, indeed, must be, if these views are given with cogent reference to the precise issues he had to decide.'[24]

Goodhart's criticism of the use of an enunciated rule as the guiding *ratio decidendi* in a later case emanates from the concern that such enunciation may be too wide or too narrow and, therefore, not made with cogent reference to the precise issues to be decided. Stone too pointed out that even the classical theory must admit the possibility that on examination the principle propounded by a judge as the necessary basis of his decision may turn out, in the opinion of a later court, to have been not sufficiently related to the holding on the facts.[25] There must then be *some* relation between such holding and the rule propounded. According to Stone, the difficulty, as we have seen, lies in the competing levels of generality of the material facts. Nevertheless, the classical theory does presuppose some relationship between the 'inferring' and the enunciation. It is not entirely independent of the material facts method.

Professor Wechsler would, moreover, require of an enunciated rule that it be 'viable in reference to applications that are now foreseeable'[26] that are foreseeable, that is, at the time the rule is formulated. Professor Levi, on the other hand, disagrees with him but demands that such rule explain the way prior cases as well as the instant case have been handled. This may be a way of stating the requirement that the enunciation be permitted or required by preexisting principles, for free rule-making is an activity very different from rule formulation arising in the process of the application of preexisting principles to factual situations.

The formulation of such a rule, we have seen, is designed to *justify* the inference drawn in the case in which it first makes its appearance, and it is also designed for use as a rule of guidance in later cases. It plays a dual role which requires that it meet some functional specifications:

1. it must be required or permitted by a preexisting rule or principle (substantially Levi's point);

2. It must justify the inference drawn in the case in which it is enunciated, it must be necessary for, or the basis of the decision (substantially Goodhart's point);

3. it must, like any other rule, be capable of being followed or applied in subsequent cases (substantially Wechsler's point);

4. it must lead, in the case in which it is formulated, to results which are compatible with the purposes and policies upheld by the courts.[27]

(iii) The rule or principle preexisting the precedent case

This theory is attributed to Salmond,

'The underlying principle . . . which forms its authoritative element is . . . the *ratio decidendi* . . . which alone has the force of law.'[28]

As Montrose points out, it assumes that there always is a rule of law for which a case is of binding authority. The significance of this theory has already been made plain. It is a preexisting rule or principle – if any – which authorize both the reasoning and the formulation of a guiding rule. In this sense, of course, the reasoning and the enunciation can be considered as evidence of preexisting rules and general propositions of which they are but particular applications.

In conclusion, it must be pointed out that the practices of courts which rely merely upon obiters and naked policy considerations to legitimize their decisions are viewed with disfavour and suspicion as the unprincipled exercise of judicial power. The three theories of *ratio decidendi* suggest that the use of precedent involves two very different though closely related techniques: the technique of reasoning with rules, either preexisting or newly formulated, and the technique of reasoning from examples (or analogy). Courts have followed both techniques and indeed, it is one of the distinguishing marks of precedent that both techniques are resorted to in a strange and fruitful amalgam. Although it would be idle to tell the courts which technique to adopt, they must nevertheless realize that each of the three techniques has its own implications and limitations. This realization has the power to prevent spurious problems. Thus, as this analysis confirms, courts need not be concerned with the argument that they are bound by a precedent court's determination that its enunciated rule is a correct *ratio* binding in later cases. It is of the essence of a rule of justification that it be open to criticism and to review, while it is of the essence of a rule of guidance that the decision on how to apply it rest in the hands of those doing the applying.

Judicial law-making

It is impossible when speaking of the law to refer to a rigid and static set of positive rules. A legal system, as distinct from a set of rules in a game, is a dynamic congeries of rules and principles in the process of application and development. The trite adjective 'organic' may indeed be most appropriate to describe such a system. The inherent mobility of legal rules reveals the quixotic character of the quest for absolute legal certainty. It is underscored by important modern juristic writings which stress the relativity of law-making and law-applying. Kelsen wrote that,

'From a dynamic standpoint, the individual norm created by the judicial decision is a stage in a process beginning with the establishment of the first constitution. . . . Statutes and customary laws are, so to speak, only semi-manufactured products which are finished only through the judicial decision and its execution. The process through which law constantly creates itself anew goes from the general and abstract to the individual and concrete.'[29]

It is the doctrine of precedent which holds the key to the mystery of how, in Lord Wright's well publicized words, '. . . this perpetual process of change can be reconciled with the principle of authority and the rule of *stare decisis*'.[30] For under this doctrine every inference drawn, and every rule enunciated warrants similar inferences in yet other cases. Each decision thus extends the family of similar cases. It allows similar inferences in situations similar to yet other situations. The doctrine of precedent, therefore, transmutes law-applying into law-making. Every inference made and every rule enunciated must be authorized or required by preexisting rules and principles, but precedent transforms that which is authorized or required into that which authorizes and requires. There is, therefore, no contradiction between the two propositions that courts always apply preexisting law and that courts create law. New rules and precedents are gradually infused into the legal system and law becomes a system which grows with use. The distinction between legal inferences, rules which warrant them and the rules freshly enunciated, is, therefore, not of logical interest only. It explains the phenomenon of the growth of the law and it refutes the old-fashioned notion that the application of a legal rule merely involves the deduction of inferences which it presupposes. But it also suggests that there is something to the sneered-at doctrine that the common-law rests 'in the bosom of the judges' from time immemorial. In a sense it does. It does to the extent that layer upon layer of decisions has grown to authorize yet other decisions derived from the earlier ones.

A state which adheres to the doctrine of precedent in either its Continental or Anglo-Saxon form, must reconcile itself to the fact that judicial law-making is an inseparable facet of law-applying, and that it will have a government of laws as well as a government of men. The doctrine of separation of powers, if strictly interpreted to require that judges not make laws, demands that the doctrine of precedent be abandoned. There is an internal contradiction between the strict doctrine of the separation of powers and the theory of precedent. In other words, the method of the common law cannot be reconciled with the doctrine that judges should not make law. Montesquieu, who inspired the authors of the American Constitution to adopt the doctrine of the separation of powers had used the British Constitution as a model. He wrote *de L'Esprit des Lois* at a time when the High Court of France, the Parlement de Paris, cited neither reason nor authority for its decisions.[31] The doctrine of the separation of powers imposes a dilemma: it requires the judiciary to write opinions since,

'To avoid an arbitrary discretion in the courts, it is indispensable that they should be bound down by strict rules and precedents, which serve to define and point out their duty in every particular case that comes before them;'[32]

and since opinions are the best method of guaranteeing judicial decision according to principle. But then it must be expected that the courts and the public at large will rely on such decisions, or at least on a string of such decisions, to determine what the law is. The strict doctrine of separation of powers requires on the other hand that judges apply the law and not make new rules, yet the only method for depriving the judiciary of its law-making powers is to require it to give no reasons and cite no authorities for its decisions, with the attendant risk of unprincipled and arbitrary decision-making and of repeated litigation of similar issues.

The freedom of judges in judicial law-making can be easily exaggerated. The demand that their decisions be principled, that the rules they enunciate meet at least the four fundamental requirements which we have outlined, would severely limit their freedom in formulating new rules. Allen thus speaks of the distinct sense in which we can speak of judges 'making' the law, and judiciously underlines the contrast with the freedom of legislatures to frame statutes without regard to past principles and decisions.[33] It is rather odd as Wolfgang Friedmann points out, that scholars and practitioners continue to be deeply divided on whether judges actually do contribute to the evolution of law.[34] But since Gény's pioneering work there is perhaps a tendency to overstate their lee-ways of choice.

The conspicuity of judicial creativeness depends to some extent on the technique used by the courts in following prior decisions. The use of precedent according to the 'material facts' method defended by Goodhart, which is perhaps more characteristic of English than American practice, requires the comparison of two sets of factual situations: those of the precedent case and those of the case to be decided. The law then grows and develops with the accretion of distinctions between different recurring situations. The emphasis of the material facts technique is on the examination and comparison of factual situations. Legislation on the other hand requires a totally different technique. The application of rules and regulations involves – as we shall see – consideration of the purposes and policies of the rules applied. The emphasis is then less on the comparison of concrete situations of fact than on the evaluation and weighing of competing policies and ends. The common law technique of reasoning on the material facts of a case tends, therefore, to divert deliberation from the purposive character of law by channelling argument to factual distinctions. On the other hand, legislative and particularly constitutional interpretation invites the clarification of policies and requires choices between values. The by-products of these techniques are pervasive and affect the ethos of a whole legal system. The one shields the courts from involvement in policy decisions and keeps the purposive functions of law well out of sight. The other exposes the courts to arguments about values and draws them closer to the political arena. In the last resort, these techniques affect the very position of the judiciary in the state.

THE INTERPRETATION OF RULES

Some concepts of interpretation

The technique of following and applying rules is, as we have suggested, quite different from the technique of reasoning by example although both are resorted to in the use of precedent. For our purposes we need not here differentiate between rules authoritatively promulgated – such as statutes – and rules enunciated by judges in their written opinions, despite manifest distinctions which are particularly apparent when a document like a constitution is involved.

The history of the interpretation of rules is a record of the successive misconceptions about the nature of law and language which have swept the jurisitic schools of the continent of Europe and the Anglo-Saxon countries. They are by no means at an end. As C. K. Allen observed, the principles of statutory interpretation are one of the less stable, less consistent and less logically satisfying branches of jurisprudence.[1] Perhaps more than any other branch of jurisprudence these principles can benefit from review in light of the method of modern linguistic analysis.

The more important fashions and doctrines of interpretation which have dominated judicial minds have been collected in a brilliant essay by C. P. Curtis.[2] It is advisable to list them one by one:

i. the interpretation of a rule depends upon the discovery of the true or plain meaning of its words. This is the so-called 'one word one meaning school';

ii. or upon the intention of the author of the rule;

iii. or upon the intention which the author would have had if he had addressed his mind to the problem;

iv. or upon anticipation of the results of an appeal involving the construction of the rule;

v. or upon the meaning which a reasonable layman would assign to the rule in the given circumstances.

Curtis' own 'Better Theory of Legal Interpretation' bears some affinity with the concept of rule advanced in this work. It is the theory that,

vi. words are but delegations of the right to interpret them and questions of interpretation turn upon whether such words have been reasonably and properly acted upon.

These theories embrace two separate sets of investigations; investigations about the rules themselves and investigations about their use. They can perhaps be examined in a brief survey as follows:

(i) *The one word one meaning school*

Curtis points out that legal interpretation was taxonomic like the classification of Latin names for flowers. It was believed that each word has and can have only one legal meaning. The paradigm for each word was the proper name, designed to apply to one object only. Words were deemed to correspond to things or objects belonging to ascertainable groups. Dictionaries were conceived as catalogues of words referring to things. Just as naming involved giving names to things, objects and creatures, so interpretation involved finding the things, object or creature corresponding to a word.

The assumption was that no competing meanings can coexist within the narrow confines of a single word. A rule of law was believed to have one meaning only, and from this rule the decision of the courts was expected to flow logically. If more than one meaning was suggested, only one meaning could be correct and the other was necessarily incorrect.[3] Interpretation was, therefore, seen as a scientific inquiry bent on discovering the truth, not on choosing the right. Kohler was among the first to expose this fallacy. He wrote that though one might at first sight take it for granted that legislation is the expression of the mind of the legislator, an act of legislation is a definite text which alone bears legislative force. If a text can be read with six different meanings, it is wrong, he argued, to say that only one meaning is true. What has been made law is not one but all the potential meanings, and the job of interpretation is the job of selecting the decisive authoritative meaning. 'A statute is an instrument for producing beneficial results, and not a social phenomenon to be examined with a view to its truth or falsity.'[4]

The early hold of the one word one meaning theory is suggested by an interesting citation from the speech of Brook C. J. in *Thockmerton v. Tracy*, a 1554 case,

'. . . the party ought to direct his meaning according to law, and not the law according to his meaning, for if a man should bend the law to the intent of the party, rather than the intent of the party to the law, this would be the way to introduce barbarousness and ignorance and to destroy all learning and diligence. For if a man was assured that whatever words he made use of his meaning only should be considered, he would be very careless about the choice of his words, and it would be the source of infinite confusion and uncertainty to explain what was his meaning.'[5]

(ii) (iii) *Intention*

There is no need to do more than mention this doctrine. It has been exhaustively discussed and it still greatly influences the construction of statutes despite the reservations of Holmes and Frankfurter.[6]

As late as the early nineteenth century the inquiry about intention was viewed with considerable misgivings, because it challenged the accepted notion that words could have only one meaning. It is reported that in 1814, Le Blanc J. considered the inquiry about intention 'a very dangerous rule to go by, because it would be to say that the same words should vary in their construction.'[7] But later, the reaction against the orthodox doctrine of interpretation took the form of an unbridled search for intention and led to the illusion that 'words in themselves have no meaning at all, and . . . we must look through them and behind them and peer into what the author intended.'[8] The search for intention led even to the fictional attribution of intention where none had existed, with Mr Justice Cardozo asking in *Burnet v. Guggenheim*, 'which choice is it the more likely that Congress would have made?'[9] It led also in the U.S. to the increasingly common manufacture of legislative history during the course of legislation with the object of influencing future court decisions.

(iv) *Anticipating appeals*

Some judges attempted to avoid the difficulties inherent in turning their courts into institutes for the study of the history of legislation. They sought guidance in anticipating what would have been decided on appeal. Thus, Judge Learned Hand wrote in a dissent in *Spector Motor Co., v. Walsh* that it is not,

'desirable for a lower court to embrace the exhilarating opportunity of anticipating a doctrine which may be in the womb of time, but whose birth is distant; on the contrary I conceive that the measure of its duty is to divine, as best it can, what would be the event of an appeal in the case before it.'[10]

Curtis also cites Judge Parker's opinion in the flag saluting case of *Barnette v. West Virginia Board of Education* as another example of the readiness of a judge to interpret the Constitution in the light not of a binding precedent but of his expectation that the Supreme Court would uphold him.[11]

(v) *The reasonable man's interpretation*

This is the position advocated by Holmes who was no adherent of the school that intention should determine interpretation. Discussing the interpretation of legal instruments he wrote in the *Harvard Law Review* that,

'It does not disclose one meaning conclusively according to the laws of language. Thereupon we ask, not what this man meant, but what those words would mean in the mouth of a normal speaker of English, using them in the circumstances in which they were used, and it is to the end of answering this last question that we let in evidence as to what the circumstances were.'[12]

Curtis observes that Holmes would have us apply to a contract the sense which a reasonable layman in the given circumstances would assign to it. Holmes, he says, is offering a laicized version of the medieval one word one meaning theory, and he objects to the notion that in interpreting we can be talking of *one* meaning as Holmes did.[13]

(vi) *The free discretion of judges*

The 'Pure Theory of Law' broke new ground when it maintained that 'no norm is completely determined by the superior norm which governs it, since between the two norms there must always be a certain degree of free discretion.' In the words of Kelsen,

'In all these cases the norm to be put into effect has only the character of a frame into which several possible applications may fit; thus any act would conform to the norm which comes within the frame.'[14]

The 'pure theory' is in conflict with the orthodox theory of interpretation – with the 'one word one meaning' school. In Kelsen's view, the right application of law, the filling of the frame, is not a matter for knowledge, but for the will and the judge cannot find legal guidance for his choice, because the law leaves the decision open among the various interests pressing. This theory views every application of law as a law-making activity, even in those cases in which application appears to be 'obvious'. The 'pure theory' ignores, however, the limitations on discretion which provided the keystone for Mr Justice Frankfurter's judicial philosophy. It does not recognise the 'vital difference' between 'initiating policy, often involving a decided break with the past, and merely carrying out a formulated policy'.[15] Kelsen's theory thus fails to provide the safeguard against crossing the line between adjudication and legislation which was of such importance to the late Justice. But it underlines the area of choice which courts possess within the framework of statutes. We shall examine in the next chapter to what extent the 'vital difference' does provide a check on judicial law-making.

Some uses of 'interpretation'

Before reviewing Curtis' own theory of interpretation it would be helpful to consider in a digression some of the occasions on which 'interpretation' is said to take place. To look, that is, at the uses of this overworked concept. The word 'interpretation' accounts for much of what is also known as the judicial process. It is the link between rules and action under rules, between inference-warrants and the inferences themselves. The difficulty with this word lies in the spectacular breadth of uses to which it has been put and the consequent erosion of meaning. It is used in connection with signs and manuscripts, concerts and paintings, theatrical performances and literary criticism, laws and nature, situations and maps, and with a score of other matters. Moreover, even within one single context its meaning drifts in a most treacherous manner. So that it can refer to obscurities in a legal text which are independent of its application, to difficulties in application as well as to the reasons for and canons of interpretation.

(i) *Interpretation: questions about facts, their appraisal and selection.* The word is used in this sense by a map reader who wishes to find out where he is located. He tries to discover something about himself, not something about the map, something about which the map is helpful, but something which would be true or false independently of any map. Interpretation is also used in this sense when we refer to the things which a painter selects for emphasis: light and the quality of light which Monet tries to render in the *Nymphéas*, or time and the quality of time which Dali conveys with clocks melting into the landscape.

(ii) *Interpretation : questions about things interpreted.* These refer to the thing interpreted, whether applied, performed or relied upon. They refer, for example, to a legal rule which requires application, to a scientific law tested in an experiment, or to a musical score to be performed. Interpretation of this nature, may concern matters such as validity, *ultra vires* and unconstitutionality, and the weight and authority of rules. In other fields, it may involve the precise formulation of a scientific law which requires testing, or the authenticity of manuscripts in historical research.

(iii) *Interpretation : questions about the application of rules.* These refer to an action, to an event like the act of applying a rule. A voyage made with the guidance of a map is an act of inference in accordance with the map. (If the lights on my right are those of Calais, those on my left are those of Dover. To sail straight ahead is such an act.) To interpret in this sense is, therefore, neither to speak of the map, nor to speak of the particular point at which we may now be. It is to speak of the journey made in accordance with the map. This is also the meaning of interpretation when we speak of a performance. A performance of the Bach Mass in B is something different from the score of the Mass itself. It is an event in which the score is, so to speak, applied. Acting a play is also an interpretation. Olivier's Hamlet must not be confused with the Hamlet of the play. We can talk of the play and of the performance and yet not talk of the same thing. We can evaluate the play and the performance differently.

The contrast between interpretations that lead to choice and those that do not also requires notice. Literary criticism can be usefully compared with legal interpretation. In his essay on *Logic and Appreciation*, Stuart Hampshire writes that a work of art is gratuitous and not essentially the answer to a question or the solution of a presented problem. He distinguishes gratuitous from moral actions,

'Compare the subject-matter and situation of moral judgment. Throughout any day of one's life, and from the moment of waking, one is confronted with situations which demand action. Even to omit to do anything positive, and to remain passive, is to adopt a policy; Oblomov had his own solution to the practical problems confronting him; his was one solution among others. . . . Action in response to any moral problem is not gratuitous; it is imposed; that there should be some response is absolutely necessary.'[16]

The distinction between interpretation that leads to appreciation and that which leads to action is essential. It is a distinction which, incidentally, does not commit us to any particular view of what a work of art is. The job of a critic is easily contrasted with that of a judge who must reach a decision. Writing of the critic, Hampshire observes that,

'Anything may be seen or heard or read in many different ways, and as an arrangement of any number of elements of different kinds. The picking out of the elements and of their pattern, in defiance of habit and practical interest, is a work of practice and skill.'[17]

A critic brings out undiscovered treasures or trivia from a work of art. He may also seek parallel meanings, and notice the plurality of levels of discourse. This is also true of the law. The law has both critics and men of action. Kelsen, for example, in his commentary on the Charter of the United Nations, assumes the role of the critic.[18] He informs his reader with painstaking neutrality of the various meanings which the individual articles of the Charter can be made to bear. He need neither act nor decide. On the other hand, a judge of the International Court, or the President of the Security Council must make his decision and stand by one interpretation, overruling all others. To take another example, Toscanini performed a passage in the scherzo of Beethoven's Seventh symphony with an animated tempo. Bruno Walter preferred to direct the same passage with a slower, more majestic rhythm. Both Toscanini and Walter must have been aware of each other's rendering. They must both have known that the score of the Seventh contains the possibility of both performances, and yet they had to choose, to decide. They were not acting as critics who can point out, inform and guide. They were performers who had to act and make the inevitable exclusion. It is evident that the activity pursued colours the character of the interpretation. The performance of Beethoven's Seventh symphony requires the exclusion of all other readings. In a sense, every artistic performance contains a tragic component, for it requires a rendition restricted to only one of many potential meanings. It requires a self-imposed limitation on the realization of meaning, which in practice often leads to the negation of other meanings. But interpretation geared to pure appreciation

G

can tolerate and does sometimes thrive on a plurality of meanings. Interpretation geared to choice must lead to action on one meaning. It must lead to decision *as if* there were but one meaning.

(iv) *Interpretation: questions about the choice between competing rules*. The decision which must be taken in such cases cannot turn on on the content of the legal rules themselves. In order to avoid a naked choice, some other rules must be resorted to. Thus the Constitution of the United States provides that in the event of a conflict between a treaty and a statute, the treaty shall prevail. This kind of difficulty is not restricted to the law-courts; a conductor may have to choose between two versions of an orchestral work; an actor may have to choose between rival editions of a play.

(v) *Interpretation: questions about what is being interpreted*. This kind of elucidation must necessarily precede any careful argument. A critic's review which fails to show whether he is concerned with a play or with the performance of the play or an argument about law reform which fails to discriminate between *lege lata* and *lege ferenda*, both confuse and lead astray.

The failure to ascertain the subject matter of discourse and its function can lead to careless inferences from one field of argument to another. Thus the fact-value dichotomy, which has been useful in some analytic studies has been invoked by Kemeny, an eminent American mathematician, to support a frightening scheme for political reform which would give immense powers to scientists in an allegedly rational state.[19] He simply applied a distinction in one field to support an argument in another, without noticing that in shifting from one field to another, the distinction ceased to apply in the same manner.

(vi) *Interpretation: questions about the choice between the criteria which determine interpretation*. Criteria such as the intention of the author, the true purpose of a statute and the true and natural meaning of words are all resorted to. To choose between them we need some conception of what interpretation is for, as well as some conception of the ends and functions of the field of discourse. This kind of interpretation moves towards an appraisal of ends, policies and purposes which are the concern of the next part of this book.

Interpretation is most challenging when it involves the jump from the domain of rules to the domain of action. It then establishes the link between guidance and action. The crucial decisions take place at this juncture even though their ultimate significance is not dealt with. When a court determines that a 'pram' is a 'vehicle' it makes its decision without working out the significance of its judgment in terms of ultimate choice, just as an ordinary citizen does not reflect on the validity of delegated legislation when he considers whether he should comply with some traffic ordinance. The part of a decision which is generally explicit, usually forms but a small part of the arguments which can be offered in its defense. Sometimes, the logical gap between law and application of law is so wide that a discussion of policies and of ultimate choices – to which we shall pay attention later – becomes necessary, and sometimes this discussion arises because the case is closely connected with these ultimate choices. Thus questions of self-defence and necessity often require a review of the practical options, as in the case of the cannibalistic shipwrecks, *R. v. Dudley and Stevenson*.[20] But fundamental choices remain latent, even when they are not in the foreground of argument. Extreme cases like *Dudley and Stevenson* just bring them out to the surface.

The confusion resulting from the elusive nature of interpretation is also at the root of some of the arguments on the relation between law and morals. In the tradition of Mill, it is usual to insist on the distinction between the law that is and the law that ought to be. This does not conflict with the contention that we must decide what the law is in the light of what it ought to be. These views are not contradictory for when we speak not of a rule but of the inferences that can be made on its authority, some conception of what the law ought to be is necessarily infused in the process of application. The hard and fast distinction between the law that is and the law that ought to be which we can draw for the purpose of legislative reform is considerably eroded when we speak of judical application.

The 'Better Theory of Interpretation'

Curtis' own theory of interpretation has affinities with Ludwig Wittgenstein's concept of rule. Curtis confines the meaning of the word 'meaning' in legal documents to applications to the particular. This suggests that the meaning of words is to be sought not in their author but in the person addressed, and,

'. . . in the defendant who is charged with violating the statute, in the conduct of any person who is acting under the authority and either within or without the authority of the words to be interpreted. Words are but delegations of the right to interpret them, in the first instance by the person addressed, in the second and ultimate instance by the courts who determine whether the person addressed has interpreted them within their authority.'[21]

Language in legal documents, therefore, does not fix meaning but circumscribes it. In many respects then, Curtis' theory of interpretation is designed to supersede the concepts of interpretation which we have briefly discussed. It is grounded on a theory of language which transcends legal problems of interpretation. It is not a theory of craft, an artisanal technique for handling statutes, but rather a philosophically backed theory which seeks to impose itself by its evident persuasiveness. His theory stresses the function of the rule after its enunciation or promulgation. The fulfilment of a rule lies in being applied. On application there is a natural tendency to read back *into* the rule as enunciated something which is really determined only upon subsequent application, to claim that is, as an attribute *of* the rule enunciated something which was not originally a part of it. So that it is common, for example, to say that a rule about vehicles 'includes' prams, although what this really means is that the rule referring to vehicles and which was perfectly silent about prams – was subsequently applied to prams. This way of speaking naturally gives rise to the impression that there is more in the original rule than meets the eye, this is very comfortable for the rule-applier who then seems to be deciding less and discovering more about the rule he follows.

We have seen that rules are inference-guidance devices and that they authorize or require a whole range of inferences which are not individually predetermined. Indeed this seems to be one of the hallmarks of rules distinguishing them from commands which contemplate particular applications in clearly anticipated circumstances. Curtis' theory of interpretation fits perfectly with this concept of rule. Since a rule permits or requires a whole range of potential inferences, the problem of applying rules – or interpreting them – is not to discover the meaning of words in the rule. The problem is entirely different,

'It is whether the person to whom the word was addressed acted reasonably in choosing and acting on the one of many meanings which he did choose and did act on. It is not simply what would a reasonable man have taken the words to mean, or what the speaker would reasonably have expected him to understand. This embodies the fallacy of the single right meaning. There is a world of difference between what a reasonable man would have done and whether a particular man acted reasonably, and not beyond the length of the tether.'[22]

The main problem of interpretation in other words is whether the inference drawn in accordance with the rule is authorized or required by such rule. Not what the meaning of words in the rule is, but whether the words authorized the inference made in reliance on them. The problem of interpretation thus entirely changes in character, it involves not discovering something in the rule, but finding guidance for the application of rules. This question, which then becomes the hard question, is not answered by Curtis who honestly admits that to answer it would call for a great work on jurisprudence, or a greater book on justice. This analysis thus leaves us with a reformulated but unresolved problem.

Canons for the construction of statutes – guidance or justification

Mr Justice Frankfurter observed that the canons of construction of statues cannot save us from the anguish of judgment. 'Such canons', he wrote, 'give an air of abstract intellectual compulsion to what is in fact a delicate judgment, concluding a complicated process of balancing subtle and elusive elements.' He pointed out that Holmes, Brandeis and Cardozo had all, at one time or another, leaned on the crutch of a canon, but that they had done so only rarely and with the recognition that these rules of construction are not in any true sense rules of law, but rather in the words of Mr Justice Holmes, 'axioms of experience'.[23] Frankfurter thus echoed the perceptive comment of Wurzel that 'laws governing interpretation are natural laws, not legal norms' presumably in the sense that they are logical or linguistic laws.[24]

Canons of construction have figured prominently in the practice of courts and their conceptual status requires clarification. Let us try to situate them. In easy cases no questions are raised about the application of rules to the facts of a case. The reason for the application needs not then be articulated. The rule 'obviously' suffices. In more difficult cases, questions arise about the inferences permitted under such rules. Under the prevailing concepts of interpretation, these questions are understood to arise in connection with the meaning of words in rules. To guide decisions about these questions, there exist in most legal systems bodies of rules for the application of rules. These rules are known as canons for the construction of statutes. They have their counterparts when similar questions arise about the applicability of precedents. It suffices here to refer to Llewellyn's brilliant analysis of the sixty-four available precedent techniques – legitimate and illegitimate – which common law judges have adopted in handling precedents.[25] For what we have here to say about the status of rules of construction applies equally to the techniques for the use of precedents.

Some of the older rules widely used in scholastic reasoning and in early statutory construction led to five broad types of interpretation,

'1. "Interpretatio extensiva", where the sense is broader than the text. 2. "Interpretatio lata", where the text is ambiguous and is liberally construed. 3. "Interpretatio declarativa", where text and meaning are co-extensive and unambigouus. 4. "Interpretatio stricta", where the text is ambiguous and is construed strictly. 5. "Interpretatio restrictiva", where the meaning is narrower than the text.'[26]

These obviously do not offer much guidance for choosing between competing interpretations. Wurzel observed that there is scarcely a rule of statutory interpretation, however orthodox, which is not qualified by large exceptions 'some of which so nearly approach flat contradiction that the rule itself seems to totter on its base'.[27] The comments of Llewellyn also run in the same direction,

'When it comes to presenting a proposed statutory construction in court, there is an accepted conventional vocabulary. As in argument over points of case-law, the accepted convention still, unhappily, requires discussion as if only one single correct meaning could exist. Hence *there are two opposing canons on almost every point*.'[28] (Emphasis added).

This, of course, is not new to lawyers, who know that they can always find some canon to support an advocated interpretation in Sutherland's three volume edition of Statutory Construction. The conclusion is inescapable: since canons compete in justification of judgment their role cannot be one of guidance.

Rules, principles and canons are an assortment of tools for the performance of the judicial task. The judge picks the tool he finds most suitable and proceeds to use it on the body of the text interpreted. Likewise, the surgeon chooses his tool in order to perform an operation. But when the surgeon is asked why he uses one tool rather than another, he answers that it is better designed for the removal of the organ operated on. On the other hand, when the judge uses canons of construction, he gives the tool as the reason for the operation he performs. If asked why he uses a particular principle of interpretation, he does not say that he intends to perform a certain kind of interpretation and that the canon selected helps him in his task. On the contrary, he would say that it is the canon which requires him to make a certain interpretation. Mr Justice Frankfurter would have us disregard such canons entirely. He argued that to strip the task of judicial reading of statutes,

'. . . of rules that partake of the mysteries of a craft serves to reveal the true elements of our problem. It defines more accurately the nature of the intellectual responsibility of a judge and thereby subjects him to more relevant criteria of criticism.'[29]

The judicial use of such canons may, however, itself fulfil a judicial purpose such as the preservation of the neutrality of judicial reasoning and the insulation of the process of interpretation from overt consideration of purposes and policies. Significantly, it is near the eye of political storms that the demand for 'neutral principles' is again heard. The canons of construction have been particularly well adapted to this end. Their protective technical colouring has not attracted much investigation. They appear too contradictory, too legalistic, too morally neutral to be capable of concealing the principal gate for the infiltration of policy choices. Just as in the application of precedents the selection of the material facts provides judges with the opportunity for exercising their choices unobtrusively and sometimes unconsciously, in statutory interpretation it is the selection of the canon of construction which provides them with a similar occasion.

Canons of construction function, therefore, not as rules of guidance but as rules of justification. We have already suggested the difference between the two kinds of rules. A rule of guidance must be capable of guiding a choice before a decision is made. It must be possible for a judge to act on it. A rule of justification enables a judge to give such rule as a reason for his decision even though he did not rely on it in reaching his decision. Rules of guidance are also rules of justification, but it can be seen in the case of canons of interpretation that not all rules of justification are also rules of guidance. A rule of justification legitimates certain 'moves' in the sense that questions about the legitimacy of these moves can be answered by reference to the rule. It does not mean, however, that the moves were made in reliance on such rules. Rules of justification can, therefore, sometimes provide a cloak which conceals the effective grounds for a decision.

When canons are used to justify rather than guide the application of statutes, another problem must logically be faced. The use of rules to determine the application of other rules can, though it need not, go on *ad infinitum*. For these canons may require yet other canons to govern their application particularly when rival canons are inexorably pressed. Wittgenstein was aware of this problem,

'. . . what does a game look like that is everywhere bounded by rules? whose rules never let a doubt creep in, but stop up all the cracks where it might? – Can't we imagine a rule determining the application of a rule, and a doubt which *it* removes – and so on?'[30]

And what would adjudication look like if it were to continue this search for rules to apply rules? Rules of justification may have their uses, but they are no substitute for rules of guidance. It is the problem of guidance for the application of rules which we must face next.

VIII

THE ROLE OF PURPOSE

The purposes or functions of a legal system

The concept of purpose has been much tossed about in recent jurisprudential storms. It is now embroiled in the debate over modern natural law. Lon Fuller has recently written that 'A statute is obviously a purposive thing, serving some end or congeries of related ends. What is objected to is not the assignment of purposes to particular laws, but to law as a whole'.[1] Yet the purpose which he attributes to the institution of law is a 'modest and sober one' that of subjecting human conduct to the guidance and control of general rules.

A different less procedural view of the function of law was taken by Wasserstrom who wrote 'I shall suppose . . . . that a desirable legal system is one that succeeds in giving maximum effect to the needs, desires, interests, and aspirations of the members of the society of which it is a part'.[2] In a discerning comment, Ronald Dworkin observed that it may well be that in our society, or any other society for that matter, 'there simply *is* no sufficient consensus on an overriding goal to say that any particular function of law forms part of the standards of the society as such'.[3] He accordingly questioned the uncritical acceptance of the utilitarian standard as the appropriate test of judicial decisions. He raised the question whether it is at all proper to test a rule of decision by its power to promote any kind of social situation rather than for representing the application of principles of fair play generally endorsed and publicized in a community. We need here go no further into this debate or into the debate about the 'minimum content of natural law' which is the content that law must have, in Hart's opinion, if there is to be any point in having rules of law at all.[4] This argument together with all considerations of the purposes of *law as a whole*, must be sharply distinguished from our use here of the concept of purpose.

The purposive character of individual rules

The use of the concept of purpose in the framework of this analysis scarcely lends itself to excesses, for we are concerned here with the purposes of single rules and enactments, and yet even this limited treatment leads to some surprising implications.

The concept of rule which we have adopted here – a device for the guidance of mental processes of inference leading to decisions and judgments – is inherently purposive. This is a truism suggesting that guidance and regulation is not an aimless activity but is designed for some end-in-view. Significantly enough, Hart who has resisted the ascendency of purpose advocated by Lon Fuller, recognizes its undisputed role in the *application* of law. He wrote that the criterion which makes a decision sound in the case of the interpretation of statutes is some concept of what the law ought to be, and he recognized that 'it is easy to slide from that into saying that it must be a moral judgment about what law ought to be'.[5] Lon Fuller emphasized that if in some cases we seem to be able to apply a rule without asking what its purpose is, this is not because we can treat a directive arrangement as if it had no purpose, but rather because we know the purpose 'without thinking'.[6] He demanded that we be sufficiently capable, when we apply a rule, to put ourselves in the position of those who drafted the rule to know what they thought the application ought to be.[7] Nothing he says on this score is contested by Hart.

Statutes have a function and so do rules of every kind. This is also implicit in Dewey's theory of judicial reasoning in which consequences rather than antecedents take the place of honour. If statutory purposes are manifest, this does not imply that individual rules of common law do not have a rationale. Statutory purposes generally belong to the forward-looking state-of-affairs-to-be-advanced kind which Dworkin views with misgivings, but surely even common law rules and principles, like the rule that special damages need not be shown in cases of slander *per se* have, or at any rate had, a purpose or policy behind them. And this is so despite the fact that they do not seek to promote novel social situations. The presupposition of function inherent in the concept of rule does not favour either stability or change despite the dynamic connotations of the word function itself. Nor is this presupposition rebutted by evidence of mechanical adherence to rules whose original *raison d'être* has been lost sight of over the hazy horizon of years. Graham

Hughes remarked that a rule does not have a purpose. 'This,' he wrote, 'is a transferred epithet by which we refer to the human purpose in framing the rule.' He then asked,

'How do we explain the development of a rule like that of the defence of common employment in the law of torts in England, where an initial, clearly articulated purpose is more and more faintly espoused until it commands general disapproval, but lingers on in a weakened, though still operative fashion until the legislature has to step in and abrogate it?'[8]

The history of the rise and decline of particular common law rules of uncertain formulation and blurred function provides numerous examples of venerable rules in search of new roles or decaying for want of a rationale. For example, the ancient doctrine of *mitior sensus* that defamatory words ought to be construed in the sense most favourable to the defendant, had at one time a significant function to perform. It was devised to limit the impact of the rule that general damages would be presumed upon proof of the publication of defamatory words. This doctrine fell into disuse when other defences for defamatory actions were developed. Contrary examples also abound of fresh functions which like hermit crabs lodge themselves in the husks of old rules. Graham Hughes cites the English criminal law procedure of preliminary inquiry conducted by a magistrate in the case of felony which had for a long time fulfilled the purpose of ensuring a detective inquiry in the absence of an organized police force. Today it serves a totally different purpose, and is considered as the bulwark of the liberty of the individual who faces an eventual trial. Particular rules of law, and complete legal institutions thus sometimes suffer a 'sea change and serve purposes strikingly opposed to their original functions'.[9] The story of these rules and institutions suggests that it is judicial conceptions of purpose which under the pressure of steady interests animate common law rules and direct their applications. The inchoate character of such rules and their frequently unarticulated function, have often effectively concealed the purposive character of the common law. Its history cannot, however, be understood without reference to these purposes which explain the flowering and decay of whole bodies of rules.

It matters little in this context whether we speak of purpose, function or policy. The use of the concepts of 'purpose' or 'policy' has the merit of drawing attention to those whose determination of purpose is authoritative while the concept of 'function' refers to rules rather than their authors. A rule may thus be harnessed to shifting purposes while a steady policy may be promoted by novel rules. The shift in purposes does not either confirm or rebut the existence of what Fuller evocatively calls the 'collaborative articulation of shared purposes'.[10] For each successive application of the same common law rule may theoretically be inspired by shifting conceptions of policy, among which there need be no coherent unity. The successive applications of statutory rules on the other hand, should be informed by the conception of purpose which had animated the legislator. It suffices for us here to observe that each application of a rule, if it is not to be a mechanical process of obeying standing orders, must be directed by some conception of what the rule is for, and it matters little for the rationality of this argument whose purpose is governing. We shall see moreover that the application of rules, without reference to function, involves a profoundly different and quite separate matter.

The role of purpose in the application of rules

The role of purpose becomes apparent in the application of rules to the particular. We saw that the problem of interpretation involves finding guidance for the choice between permissible applications of rules, and that words in legal documents are but delegations of the authority to interpret them. The role of purpose is to provide such guidance. Let us now examine how purpose can guide the application of rules in two distinct contexts:

a. when the event to which the rule may be applicable falls within the penumbra of meaning of the words in the rule, and b. when the event to which the rule seems to apply falls squarely within the core of the meaning of such words.

To illustrate the second situation first, we can refer once more to the 'no vehicles' rule prohibiting the access of vehicles to the park. It would certainly seem to apply to a truck in perfect working order. But can we afford to pay no heed to the purpose of the rule even when the facts seem to fall within the language of the rule? Fuller raised the question: what if some local patriots wanted to mount on a pedestal in the park a truck used in the Second World War, while other citizens, regarding the proposed memorial as an eyesore, oppose its erection on the authority of the 'no vehicles' rule?[11] Surely in such a case it would be somewhat arbitrary to apply the rule in order to exclude the truck, for the rule was clearly not devised to control the erection of monuments. To invoke it in these circumstances would be to allow a decision to be guided by a rule which accidentally happens to refer to 'vehicles'. Accidentally, that is because the rule was not designed for such circumstances.

Purpose can thus be used to *preclude* the application of a rule in situations which seem to fall squarely within its language when such application would lead to results entirely alien to its purpose. This conclusion carefully argued by Fuller satisfactorily disposes of Hart's assertion that legal arguments and legal decisions of penumbral questions are the *only* occasions on which some determination of the purpose of a rule is required.

The other situation involves the question of the penumbra of meaning. When an occurrence falls within the so-called penumbra of meaning of words in a rule, it is generally admitted that reference to the purpose of the rule is required to determine whether the occurrence should be governed by it. The purpose is then used to determine the inclusion or exclusion of marginal occurrences. Thus the applicability of the 'no vehicles' rule to roller-skates or to toy automobiles would depend upon whether the rule is designed to preserve quiet in the park or to protect children and carefree strollers from injury.

It is characteristic of purposes of this order, that they do not involve grand considerations or moral policies and dilemmas. They function as unglamorous aids to decision, for the guidance of choices between rival applications of rules. But if modest rules have modest purposes, more fundamental rules, like the rules contained in the U.S. Constitution, have more fundamental purposes. But even such fundamental purposes are then attributable to the rules themselves rather than to the legal system as a whole, just as the purposes of peace and quiet in the park are attributable to the 'no vehicles' rule. These are not the purposes of morality but of rules of law. Judges need not refer to moral standards to ascertain the purposes of legal rules and principles however broad and general such legal rules and principles may be. Fundamental rules of law are not experiments in aimless direction. They presuppose congeries of purposes and policies which they are designed to promote.

The elusiveness and proliferation of purposes

The difficulty with the use of purpose for the resolution of

problems about the application of rules is their frequent indeterminacy of aim.[12] Rules and statutes are, however, no less frequently
accompanied by reasonably clear indications of what they are designed to accomplish. The purpose which a court must then
effectuate is that which the legislature *did* enact, however ineptly,
because as Mr Justice Frankfurter has put it, 'it may fairly be said
to be imbedded in the statute, even if a specific manifestation was
not thought of, as is often the very reason for casting a statute in
very general terms'.[13] When the purpose of a statute is not directly
displayed in the particular enactment, the judicial task is then
enormously complicated by the need to consider affiliated statutes
or other evidences of policy. We must, however, distinguish between difficulties in the ascertainment of the general purpose or
policy of a piece of legislation and the difficulty of ascertaining how
the legislature would have applied the statute in the particular
circumstances. We have already suggested that this second mode of
putting the question is improper, for legislation must not be confused with the disposition of particular cases. Curtis has shown the
fallacy involved in the search for the legislature's intention about
the application of statutes to particular cases. The consideration of a
statute as a means for the achievement of some ends-in-view does
not require advance decisions about its applications. We must distinguish in other words between the *purpose of a rule*, and the
application of a rule guided by such purpose. It is much easier to
find legislative intent about the former than about the latter. For,
as we must repeat, statutes contemplate delegation of the authority
to apply them.

Even so, the determination of the purpose or policy of an enactment often involves the consideration of complex compromises and
indeterminate goals which leave the legislator's policy unresolved.
Because of their vagueness, these purposes and policies cannot
function as effective guides for the application of a rule to particulars. The discretion of a court or other persons applying the
enactment is then necessarily augmented. For it is one of the functions both of the rule and the purpose to limit such discretion. The
rule limits discretion by directing what must be done in determined
circumstances, and the purpose by guiding the application of the
rule to the particular in a manner calculated to achieve the rule's
end-in-view. Accordingly, generality of rule or vagueness of purpose merely enlarge the discretion of those relying on them for
guidance.

The difficulties arising in the use of purpose for guiding the application of rules are admittedly considerable. They are compounded in the case of common law rules in which, as we have already observed, both the verbal formulation and the rationale of the rule are in a constant state of flux. In the case of promulgated legislation the administration of policy is somewhat less arduous for ends are usually authoritatively formulated. Nevertheless, it bears repeating that even the rules of the common law have functions. Remember the example of a rule without a purpose – a sign in a pond which provides 'do not tie boats to sign'.

The greatest difficulties of all arise from the proliferation of purposes. When a purpose is vaguely formulated, it readily lends itself to reformulation. This feature was underscored by Lon Fuller who argued that the meaning of any given purpose is always controlled by latent purposes in interaction with it.[14] He is fond of an evocative illustration of Wittgenstein,

'Someone says to me: "Shew the children a game." I teach them gaming with dice, and the other says "I didn't mean that sort of game." Must the exclusion of the game with dice have come before his mind when he gave me the order ?'[15]

Dewey held a substantially similar view about the unfolding character of ends-in-view, denying the possibility of fixed ends. He wrote that, 'Ends are, in fact, literally endless, forever coming into existence as new activities occasion new consequences. "Endless ends" is a way of saying that there are no ends – that is no fixed self-enclosed finalities.'[16]

The reformulation of purpose is especially warranted in the common law, where rules are not assigned specific ends by authoritative fiat. But it would be candid to recognize that purposes which undergo such 'reformulation' are substantially changed. Thus the fate of cases involving the rule about the bona fide purchaser for value discloses that it was made to do many jobs.[17] But ends-out-of-view are really *different* from, though related to, ends-in-view. The choice between related purposes is an aspect of the proliferation of purposes. We may call it 'vertical proliferation'. Thus the 'no vehicles' rule may be designed – to quote from its preamble – 'for the preservation of quiet in the parks', or it may be designed – to quote from its legislative history – 'for making parks and their neighbourhoods better and more beautiful areas'. The choice between these two formulations of policy may well determine the outcome of the case involving the truck memorial, although admittedly the first formulation of purpose is an inherent aspect of the second. The important feature of these two statements is that a choice between them may be required to decide on the application of a rule.

Moral rules, like common law rules, are neither enacted nor promulgated. The rule that 'one ought to tell the truth' may be used to uphold a variety of moral ends – to preserve trust in personal relations, or to preserve a certain mode of being. This is not surprising, for we have already seen how it is possible to have changing or multiple policies behind a static rule. Here again a choice between different formulations of purpose may be required. A determination of what exactly the rule is to be used for in the particular case may decide its application.

There is also what we may call the 'horizontal proliferation' of purposes. This involves consideration of the consequences of the application of a rule not only in terms of its own ends, but also in terms of the purposes and policies generally upheld by the system. These are not the purposes latent in a rule, but the purposes actively canvassed and promoted by other rules in force. This is sometimes known as 'consistency with the rest of the law'. This excerpt from Curtis puts the problem clearly,

'It is fair to ask what criteria I should expect the courts to apply when they come to answer this question, whether the addressee [of a rule] has acted reasonably, whether he has abused his discretion, whether he has exceeded his authority, or however you want to put the question which would be presented to the courts. . . . Personally I believe that the most important criterion is simply consistency with all the rest of the law . . . . though Justice has higher aims, the virtue on which the Law stakes its hopes of salvation is consistency.'[18]

Every concrete application of a rule leads to specific consequences which may or may not be compatible in fact with the purpose of the rule so applied. Moreover, such consequences may also be incompatible with the purposes of other rules which belong to the system of rules which it is the job of a court to apply. In making a rule it is proper for a legislator to have the purpose of *that* rule primarily in mind. In applying a rule it is necessary to consider the consequences of the application also in terms of the purposes of the other rules of the system. Any single purpose is an incomplete thing when severed from the total system of which it forms a part. For example, the 'no vehicles' rule could be invoked by a policeman to block the entrance of an ambulance rushing to the rescue of an injured child in the park. The consequence of such an action is clearly incompatible with the policy behind the whole body of law designed to promote the safety of individuals.

In hard cases, the degree of proliferation of purposes among which a choice must be made becomes menacing indeed. It may envelop a variety of purposes, from those of the individual rule to the purpose of promoting justice and maintaining the integrity and proper functioning of the legal system. For example, the purpose of the rule of construction that words in a statute should be given their ordinary meaning may be understood in terms of the interest in maintaining the integrity of the legal system, a system in which rules are devised to mould the conduct of those relying upon them for guidance. There are additional latent purposes connected with it; that no one shall be punished under laws the meaning of which is so capricious and obscure that reliance upon them becomes a matter of the greatest difficulty.

There is yet another mode of proliferation of purposes, which we may call 'parallel proliferation'. It arises when competing rules are alleged to govern a case. A determination is then necessary of the rule which is to prevail. Now, in this case as in the case of the application of a single rule, consideration of the purpose of each rule would govern the scope of its application. In these circumstances the need arises to weigh and balance these purposes as well as those arising in 'horizontal proliferation'.

To sum up, this analysis points to the pivotal role of the choice between purposes in connection with the *application* of rules to the particular. Such choice becomes necessary (i) when the situation governed by a rule is marginal with respect to the language of the rule (this is the so-called penumbral question) or (ii) when the application of a rule would be inappropriate in light of the rule's own purposes or of other preferred purposes promoted by other rules of the system; (iii) it is also necessary when competing rules claim to govern the same situation for their respective purposes must then be considered. In such circumstances it is necessary to consider purposes, in the sense that failure to do so would lead to inconsistent results in the application of rules and the disregard of their essential characteristic of purposiveness. Difficulties in these choices arise with the inherent proliferation of purposes. But such

H

proliferation, while it complicates the choice, does not alter its character. Such choice between competing purposes becomes then the next logical step in the application of rules in the three sets of circumstances we have contemplated. In other, ordinary circumstances, which generally means in the overwhelming majority of cases, rules can be applied without difficulty and without reference to the ends or the policies behind them. And by 'ordinary circumstances' we mean those which are not included in the three sets just mentioned.

These circumstances may recur more persistently in the case of the rules of common law, for both the formulation and the rationale of these rules, as we have observed, are subject to a fresh restatement with almost each reasoned application. In this regard the rules of morality resemble the rules of common law, and the problems of their application are similar. For so far as these rules are concerned – which have neither definitive formulation nor legislative statements of policy behind them – there is a greater uncertainty about what is marginal with respect to their terms and what is incompatible with their ends. This merely means that the scope of the discretion of those applying them is enlarged since the guidance which rule and purpose then provide is less precise and secure.

Purpose and the distinction between commands, rules and policy

The recognition of the role of purpose in the application of rules paves the way to an understanding of the crucial distinctions between rules on the one hand and orders and commands on the other. These distinctions go back to the concept of rule which we have adopted – rules as inference-guidance devices leading to judgments and choices. In this chapter we have in effect added to this definition the further ingredient of purposiveness. We look at rules as devices designed to guide inferences leading to choices and judgments which tend to promote some end-in-view. We have seen that rules necessarily delegate the authority to interpret them, and that considerations of purpose may have to be made also by those who apply them. Moreover, we distinguished between rules of guidance and rules of justification. Rules of guidance are used to reach a decision rather than to justify a decision already taken. We have also pointed out that all guidance devices limit the freedom of the deciding subject who is expected to rely on them. Again, we have suggested that the reasons for relying on or following a rule are logically independent and may range from the fear of sanctions to a genuine desire to follow such guidance irrespective of the absence of coercion of any kind.

In this analysis however we have so far disregarded orders and commands which we have treated here as synonymous with rules. These two notions are also used as inference-guidance devices and they are, therefore, functionally related to the concept of rule. Thus the command 'attention' given to a soldier is designed to make him do something in reliance on the comand. If the soldier snaps to attention upon hearing the command, his action involves some mental occurrence however unconscious or automatic. The soldier is not physically pushed into standing at attention; he is ordered to do so. We need not now go over the ground covered in an earlier chapter about what is meant by relying on a rule. Much of what we said there about rules applies also to orders. Thus before we can follow a rule we must determine its applicability. When we are confronted with an order, the question whether it applies or not is usually easily answered, although here again grammatical form does not tell all. For example, a sergeant may tell a soldier in his platoon 'shoot this man' or 'go to hell'. Grammatically there is not much to distinguish these two sentences and yet only one of them may be an order. An order presupposes that the addressee (i) recognizes it as an order and (ii) that it be addressed to him and also that (iii) it be valid. No more is needed for a man to act on an order which is otherwise comprehensible. Admittedly there may be marginal cases in which a soldier may doubt that an order was given – the sergeant may tell him 'give me ten dollars' – or that it was addressed to him – 'hey you there, straighten your back' – or whether the order was valid – his sergeant may tell him 'shoot the captain, this is an order'. In *these* respects, to obey an order is very much like relying on a rule.

The distinction between the two lies elsewhere, it lies in the consideration to be given to purposes in the application of commands and of rules. The concepts of order or command do not presuppose the delegation of the authority to interpret them in the light of their purposes. On the contrary, an order presupposes simple obedience on the part of the addressee who definitely has no business looking into the policy lying behind it. Thus although when we apply a rule we can legitimately inquire about what it is for, the same cannot be said of an order. It is, therefore, somewhat misleading to equate following a rule and obeying an order as

Wittgenstein did.[19] This is not to say that orders and commands are not given with some end-in-view but rather that the consideration of these ends is the exclusive concern of the commander. The recruit is not supposed to weigh matters of policy. For example, a colonel calls his officers and tells them, 'I have received a directive from HQ to pacify this area and to restore peace and quiet here. I have, therefore, decided to have the troublemakers shot. I now direct the Captain to arrest and shoot the President of the Students' Union'. The captain knows what the order is designed to achieve. He also believes that to obey the order would lead to the very opposite result. But 'an order is an order' and he obeys. He carries out the command with full knowledge that the probable consequence will be further rioting and unrest. Had the captain been given a directive rather than an order he may have felt authorized to consider the effect of the proposed execution on the policy of pacification.

Standing orders belong to the same category of inference-guidance devices. They may be couched in more general language than specific orders for immediate action. Such standing orders are designed however to trigger obedience upon the occurrence of certain events. Thus a ballistic attack on a U.S. base in Germany may call for the automatic launching of Polaris missiles. The addressee of the order is not expected to be cognizant with the policy behind it, but merely to do as he is told, to launch the missile upon the happening of certain events. A 'doomsday machine' does not follow a rule, it is designed to carry out standing orders.

The fundamental difference between obeying orders and applying rules boils down, therefore, to the extent to which purposes should be considered by the addressee. Where orders are given, the consideration of policies is the exclusive prerogative of the person in command; where rules are involved, the consideration of policies arises at two levels: at the level of legislation and at the level of application to the particular.

The concept of command involves moreover a hierarchical relationship between superior and inferior. It is also the basis of John Austin's theory of law, '. . . every law properly so called is set by a superior to an inferior or inferiors.'[20] Taking the model of the British Constitution he thus considered the 'Queen in Parliament' to be the Sovereign of Great Britain and the courts to be subordinated to this supreme composite body. This hierarchical model does not quite fit the U.S. Constitution. Learned Hand recently reminded us that under the Constitution the three departments of government were intended to be coequal 'each being as it were, a Leibnitzian monad, looking up to the Heaven of the Electorate, but without any mutual dependence'.[21] The hierarchical concept of the state, in which laws are assimilated to commands is rife with military metaphors. It has led Austin into difficulties, discussed elsewhere, when he attempted to distinguish between the 'two species' of commands: laws and rules from 'occasional or particular commands'. His proposed distinction turned on the specificity of the command, on the generality of its *protasis*,

'According to the line of separation which I have now attempted to describe, a law and a particular command are distinguished thus: – Acts or forbeareances of a *class* are enjoined *generally* by the former. Acts *determined specifically* are enjoined or forbidden by the latter.'[22]

We must stress in conclusion that the hierarchical model of the state inhibits consideration of purpose and policy in the application of laws and that the command model of legal rules tends to blur the difference between the profoundly distinct techniques involved in the use of commands and of rules.

At the other end of the spectrum we must consider the distinction between using policy and using rules as guidance-devices for reasoning. A policy, no less than an order or a rule, is designed as an inference-guidance device, and like all such devices it limits the discretion of those to whom it is addressed. By a limitation of discretion we refer to the necessary effect of all guidance techniques. Free discretion by way of contrast, involves a choice unbounded by external or public considerations. In this sense both rule and policy do not merely guide but also limit discretion and tend to exclude private prejudice as a proper ground for choice and judgment.

The source of these policies in a legal system is not always easy to pin down. It is thus possible to speak in terms of the 'values' postulated for a legal system, as Myres McDougal urges us to do.[23] Alternatively, Wolfgang Friedmann suggests that policy can be discovered in a number of sources: in the general state of legislative policy, in the state of organization in that society and in the groupings and pulls of the major social forces.[24] These, however, must be seen in the context of a pluralistic society and of the practical options open when considering available scientific techniques. In writings emanating from Yale, there has been an attempt to play down the significance of rules in the legal system, and to underscore the role of value-oriented and result-oriented arguments. For example, in his criticism of Herbert Wechsler's plea for neutral principles, Dean Rostow of Yale wrote,

'To me, Professor Wechsler's lecture . . . . represents a repudiation of all we have learned about law since Holmes published his *Common Law* in 1881, and Roscoe Pound followed during the first decade of this century with his path-breaking pleas for a result-oriented, sociological jurisprudence, rather than a mechanical one. It would raise the element of rules, of precedent, of what he calls "principle" or "reason" in the judicial process to a position of absolute primacy which all we know about law denies.'[25]

It is immaterial, from this perspective, what the sources of purposes or policies happen to be, whether they are found in specific rules or abstracted from the pull of social forces. For our concern is the quality of guidance that purposes and policies –irrespective of their origin – provide for the drawing of inferences. Ronald Dworkin has recently discussed some of the distinctions between the use of rules and of policies. Policies, he reminded us, are designed to guide inferences towards fixed results or ends-in-view. Rules, we have seen, contemplate specific settings of application and fixed conclusions designed to promote definite purposes. (Rules of a game may not always meet this last requirement.) They provide, therefore, a relatively firm guidance not only with respect to the ends to be desired but also as to the means to be adopted; they elaborate what has to be done, when and to what end.

The reasoning appropriate to decision in terms of policies differs, therefore, from the reasoning required by rules. When only policies are available to direct decisions, their executants are free to determine when and what to do provided that their decisions lead to the required goals. Policies contemplate, therefore, the delegation of a considerable degree of authority to their executants and presuppose a correspondingly significant area of indeterminacy in measures to be adopted. Where firmer and more specific guidance is needed, the adoption of rules may be advisable. For example, at the park entrance a notice announces: 'Pursuant to law, the police are authorized to enforce the following policy: to secure a quiet park, to secure a safe park, to secure a clean park.' This method of ordering would give the police a considerable degree of discretion to exclude crying babies, radios, baseball games or even smoking from the park. It would leave the public in a corresponding degree of uncertainty as to permissible activities. It is, however, possible to reduce the discretion of the police and the uncertainty of the public by a notice stating: 'No vehicles, no music, no ball playing.' Another notice may reduce these even more: 'No motorized vehicles, no radios, no ball playing except by children aged six years or less.'

It is easy to exaggerate the contrast between rule and discretion. Ronald Dworkin has elegantly challenged the widespread assumption that these are the only two sources of judicial decision.[26] Indeed it can be shown that commands, rules and policies each preclude complete discretion, in the sense that they set a limit to authorized or required behaviour. It can, however, also be shown that none of these can entirely exclude discretion, although the discretion of the recipient of a command is clearly less than that of an addressee of a rule or of the executant of a policy.

Purpose and policy, we must repeat, become relevant in the application of rules only in the three sets of circumstances previously outlined. And this perhaps is where we diverge from the so-called Yale view. Policies do not in a legal system apply directly to facts but govern the application of rules to these facts. The tendency to regard law not as a 'mere' body of rules but rather as a policy-oriented process of decision represents an extreme reaction to the command model of law. It claims for courts and lawyers a latitude of discretion undreamt of a century ago. The adoption of a particular theory of law, law as command (Austin), or law as process and policy (Lasswell and McDougal)[27] is, therefore, pregnant with implications for legal reasoning. Yet in this work we are not concerned with legal reasoning as a form of merely obeying commands, nor with legal reasoning as form of executing policy. Our concern, we must repeat is reasoning with rules generally. Such reasoning necessarily leads to the consideration of choices between purposes and policies, but it postpones these to the scrutiny of authorized or required applications of rules to the particular.

LAW AND THE CONFLICT
BETWEEN LAW AND MORALITY

The demarcation between legal rules and other rules

The concept of rule is not as perplexing as Hart suggests when studied in a functional setting. Rules, alongside with commands, orders, instructions, regulations, principles and the like are designed to guide and direct inferences leading to judgments and decisions. The identification of legal rules as a sub-species of rules advances our understanding; it calls for the articulation of a *demarcation* line between legal and non-legal rules. This demarcation is required not for abstract taxonomic reasons but for the *practical purpose* of telling which rules are applied and enforced by the machinery of a state. Hart succinctly illustrates in the *Concept of Law* the variety of laws, and the difficulties of compressing them into a single mould; legal rules which provide for the exercise of private or public legal powers, like the formation of contracts, the preparation of wills and the enactment of legislation, are very different indeed from the rules of criminal law which are more like orders backed by the threat of sanctions. On the other hand, rules such as the rules of statutory interpretation have no clear sanctions contemplated to secure their enforcement. The English system of common law also recognises certain species of custom as incorporated into the body of law applied by courts, so that the demarcation between law and non-law cannot be formulated in terms of the existence of a rule-making organ. The demarcation has for a long time been attempted – and criticised – in terms of the coercive nature of the legal order. Such demarcation is certainly not used by the law-applying organs themselves, and suggests a criminal law paradigm of law generally. But the demarcation problem is transformed when viewed in the context of the concept of rule. It is then no longer a question of defining law, but of *identifying* the rules which are considered by the state organs to belong to the system it administers. This function of identification is discharged by special rules which govern the recognition of legal rules as legal or at least as rules of the system. These rules of identification, or rules of recognition, are significantly resorted to *only when* the legal character of a particular rule is challenged. They are rules about the status of rules. In revolutionary situations like the Rhodesian rebellion, citizens and judges alike are torn between two rival authorities asserting legislative prerogatives, one in Rhodesia, the other in London. What this situation represents in jurisprudential terms is a competition between two sets of rules of recognition primarily for the loyalty of judges and other state organs. A revolution often involves the modification of the rules of recognition of a state system otherwise than in conformity with a prior set of secondary rules.[1] The change of secondary rules generally affects the legal status of only a few enactments. They act on the *periphery* of a legal system. These rules of recognition play, therefore, a peculiarly circumscribed role: Graham Hughes has clearly indicated the limited impact of such rules in territories like Norway under Nazi domination where the obedience of the bulk of the population to the general body of the laws of Norway was in no way affected by the imposition of the despised Quisling regime and the rule of recognition characterising certain acts of his regime as legal acts.[2] The 'persistency of law', to use Hart's phrase, was in no way affected by the changed rule of recognition.

This analysis identifying rules as legal when they are so recognized by secondary rules (to use Hart's terminology) raises an obvious question: what is it that characterizes the secondary rules of recognition themselves as legal? Are higher order rules required to identify these secondary rules as legal? Or, in Kelsen's words, how is it that law regulates its own creation?[3] A Wittgenstein metaphor yields the answer, '. . . it is rather, like the case of orthography which deals with the word "orthography" among others without then being second-order.'[4]

There is indeed no practical *need* to identify these secondary rules as legal or as anything else, since those relying on them know exactly what they are for, and turn to them for the purpose of identifying the status of a rule whose quality of 'legalness' is in dispute.

Another example can be derived from international law. The question whether international law is 'law' which has vexed and perplexed generations of students dissolves when approached from this perspective. The demarcation between international law and custom depends upon the secondary rules of the organ making the distinction. Thus Article 38 of the Statute of the International Court of Justice (I.C.J.) provides that,

'The Court, whose function is to decide in accordance with international law such disputes as are submitted to it, shall apply:

a. international conventions, whether general or particular, establishing rules expressly recognized by the contesting states;

b. international custom as evidence of a general practice accepted as law;

c. the general principles of law recognized by civilized mankind;

d. subject to the provisions of Article 59, judicial decisions and the teachings of the most highly qualified publicists of the various nations, as subsidiary means for the determination of rules of law.'

This article formulates the rules for the identification of the law to be applied by the I.C.J. It is itself international law by virtue of its own section (a). It indicates that there is a difference, from the viewpoint of the Court, between custom and general practice regarded as law. That is, between practices which should be applied by the Court and those which it should disregard. Now, when it comes to identify what is international law, U.S. domestic courts which 'incorporate' international law, may resort to different rules of recognition. Indeed, it would seem that international law is not quite the same body of law when viewed from the perspective of the I.C.J. and when viewed from that of an American court. Thus unanimous resolutions of the General Assembly of the United Nations which declare general principles of law may be applied as international law by the I.C.J. pursuant to Art. 38, but they are not necessarily international law as incorporated into the domestic law of the United States. In 1946, the General Assembly of the United Nations unanimously affirmed, 'The Principles of International Law Recognized by the Charter of the Nürnberg Tribunal and the Judgment of the Tribunal.'[5] This affirmation has the effect contemplated in Art. 38 of the Statute of the Court, to which incidentally the United States is a party. It does not mean, however, that it now necesarily also forms part of what American courts would treat as international law. (It should be noted, however that Art. 38 is part of U.S. law under the supremacy clause of the Constitution.) The rule of recognition characterizing international law may, therefore, vary with the forum making the determination. The use of the rule of recognition is therefore directed to determine what the law of the *forum* is.

When questions about rival sets of rules of recognition arise, the practical question 'which prevails' cannot be answered by reference to other rules. It can only be answered in terms of the actual practice of various organs, including that of the courts themselves.[6] It is then proper to speak of a rule of recognition as being *in force* in a given territory. The question 'which rule of recognition ought to prevail?' cannot be answered by reference to other rules of recognition, since to function as such each set of rules of recognition itself requires that it be followed with fidelity. It can only be answered by reference to extra-legal arguments about legitimacy.

There are still states which apply religious and positive law indiscriminately. In Saudi Arabia for example, there is not much point in fixing the line of demarcation between religious and legal rules since they all belong to the system of laws applied in state organs. The practical problem of demarcation arises only when there are doubts whether certain rules belong to the body of rules so applied. Rules of baseball, rules of etiquette, rules of religious ritual, can theoretically all become legal rules in the sense that they can all be directly followed, enforced or applied by state organs by virtue of suitable rules of recognition. It may very well be that there simply is *no* problem of demarcation apart from such practical context. To talk of the demarcation between 'law' and non-law in the abstract, is perfectly pointless. For example, the status of the constitutional conventions of the United Kingdom like the convention that the Queen must give her assent to Acts passed by both Houses of Parliament is obscure;[7] it would seem that such conventions are not 'law' under the rules of recognition of the British legal system, but they appear to be quasi-legal rules in the sense that they are followed and relied upon by the various organs of the British State, except for the law courts. This example suggests that there are degrees of 'legalness' of rules, to coin another horrible word, and that some rules may be followed and applied by the Executive and the Legislature although in the event of a dispute they will not necessarily be applied by the Courts. The inducement for relying upon such quasi-legal rules may then not lie in the implied threat of enforcement through the machinery of the courts but in the balance of political power between the different branches of the Government. The determination of the status of a rule has, therefore, clear functional implications.

This analysis does not disclose what is meant by the statement that 'a legal system exists'. It may well be that such a statement refers to patterns of social and political organization and behaviour. Rather, in talking of rules, we here analyse their nature, functions, structure, presuppositions, contexts and the distinguishing marks between different categories of rules.

An alternative to Legal Positivism and the Natural Law position on the conflict between law and morals

The theory that every legal rule is designed to promote some purpose and policy, and that consideration of such purpose and policy is the legitimate concern not only of the law-maker but of the law-applier as well, is pregnant with serious implications. One of these is that courts which apply rules, as distinct from orders or commands, necessarily have the power of judicial review over legislation and that this power is inherent in the very nature of applying rules and does not depend upon a grant of constitutional power to this effect.

Under this theory, rules of recognition no less than other rules, must be followed and applied by state organs in light of the purposes for which they are designed. Rules of recognition – which demarcate between the rules that must be followed and applied and the other rules which do not belong to the legal system – themselves belong to the legal order. This does not indicate that their purposes and functions are clearly articulated or easily ascertained, any more so than those of the galaxies of other rules and conventions which provide for example, for the qualification and election of legislators, for the appointment of judges and for the enactment procedures of legislation. They are all designed to attain some of the most delicate, elusive and fundamental goals of any legal system. And this is so whether or not there exists a written constitution or other formal declaration of purpose. These purposes are presupposed, or embedded so to speak in the 'secondary rules' of a legal system.[8] These purposes, however, are the purposes of *legal* rules so that it is not necessary to refer here to moral rules and their ends.

The heat of the debate about the legal validity of laws which violate fundamental moral principles has been such that a set of polarized positions have crystallized. We are trying here to get away from the dichotomous positions of natural law and legal positivism. We are trying to release the tight grip of the alternatives which have been pressed on this point.

Hart has examined in *The Concept of Law* 'two rival' theories of law. The first, identified with legal positivism, treats as 'law' all rules which meet the formal tests of a system of primary and secondary rules even though some of these laws do violence to a society's own standards of morality or to other views of morality which courts are pressed to abide by. The second theory, identified with Natural law, excludes from 'law' all such morally offensive rules.[9] Hart impliedly suggests that there is no third option and that one must adopt either of these two theories. He pointed out that under the positivistic view there is no logical restriction on the content of the rule of recognition which could theoretically provide that laws should cease to be regarded as such should they prove to be morally objectionable. The objection to such a theoretical arrangement would be, he felt, not logic but the gross indeterminacy of such a criterion of legal validity.[10]

Our objection to Hart's treatment of this subject is that his dichotomy is artificial and that it leaves no room for a *different* mode of dealing with legislation which meets the formal tests of the rule of recognition of a system, and which is at the same time fundamentally outrageous to the moral sense of a community.

Essentially under the alternative excluded by Hart's dichotomy we would consider as ineffective the enactment of laws which are fundamentally inimical to the purposes and goals promoted by the rules of recognition and other fundamental legal rules of the system. As Lon Fuller observed, men do not generally do absurd things that would destroy the whole undertaking in which they are engaged even though the formal directions under which they operate permit these absurdities.[11] Let us suppose, for example, that a legislature duly enacts a law which restricts suffrage to designated individuals. This law would be so destructive of the purposes of the rules for the very election of legislatures and of the purposes of the rule of recognition that questions would arise about its validity. These questions can be resolved only by reference to the rule of recognition. This means that in the case of an extreme enactment – extreme that is by reference to proclaimed purposes – the rule of recognition must be *applied* by the courts to determine whether such an enactment meets the test of that rule of recognition for belonging to the system of 'laws'. Now, the application of the rule of recognition, like the application of all other rules, cannot be made in disregard of the ends for which it is designed. Both Hart and Fuller have indicated that the *application* of a rule to the particular requires the consideration of what the rule is for.[12] To apply then the rule of recognition so as to allow the introduction into the legal system of rules destructive of the very ends and purposes which the rule of recognition is designed to promote, would be a self-contradictory and, therefore, absurd enterprise. It would be to tolerate a judicial trojan horse doctrine; it is no more absurd to prevent an ambulance from reaching an injured child in a park on the authority of a rule excluding all vehicles from the park which is expressly designed for the 'protection and safety of users of the park, especially children'. *Rules of recognition no less than rules excluding vehicles from parks, must be applied with a view to the ends they are designed to promote.* There is even less justification for tolerating the mechanical interpretation of such basic rules than there is for allowing it elsewhere. This involves however an unfamiliar argument.

Let us give a more detailed example: the Constitution of Mythaca provides in the Preamble that, 'The people of Mythaca are determined to make laws for the welfare and happiness of all the people, and, therefore, resolve to elect an Assembly giving equal representation to every citizen for the purpose of making such laws.' Article I of the Constitution grants 'all legislative powers to the Assembly to be elected by Mythacan citizens under an Election Law to be drawn up by the Framers of the Constitution'. Article II of the Constitution provides that 'The Courts of Mythaca shall interpret the Constitution and Laws of Mythaca so as to give effect to the purposes which they are designed to promote'. The Election Law was duly enacted and it provided for 500 electoral districts with equal voting power. Twenty years later, the Purity Party which had gained control of the Assembly, secured the passage of the Election Law Amendment Act which provided that, 'Whereas the urbanites have sunk into crime and depravity, and to secure the survival of truth and decency in Mythaca, be it hereby enacted that: Article I: The size of designated urban constituencies is hereby modified to contain double the number of registered voters of designated rural constituencies as follows:...' In an appeal before the Supreme Court of Mythaca, plaintiff alleged that the Election Law Amendment Act which had admittedly been duly enacted had nevertheless failed to become law. He argued that this Act was passed pursuant to the legislative powers of the Assembly under Art. I of the Constitution and that one of the purposes of the Constitution, including Art. I, as stated in the Preamble, is to give equal representation to every Mythacan voter in elections to the Assembly for the making of laws. He claimed that the Assembly could not then enact a Statute defeating the purpose for which it had been established and that Art. I could not be interpreted to recognise as 'law' enactments which would defeat its very purposes, for Art. II made it quite impossible to interpret the Constitution in disregard of its own stated ends.

The Attorney General objected that the courts of Mythaca had never exercised the power of judicial review over the Acts of the Assembly and that such power was not contemplated in the Constitution. He objected that the Court was in effect asked to assert the supremacy of the judicial department over the legislative in disregard of the clear constitutional design to create one sovereign branch namely, the legislature. Although Art. I authorized the courts to disregard non-legislative indications of the Assembly's will expressed in resolutions, it required them to apply all enactments duly passed irrespective of their content. The Constitution clearly contemplated that the authority of the legislature should be final as to when it has itself overstepped the borders of its authority and that such decision should not be open to review by another branch.

The Supreme Court allowed the appeal holding that the Election Amendment Act was not unconstitutional but that it had nevertheless failed to become law under the rule of recognition of Mythaca that the enactments of the Assembly duly passed are the law of the land. The Court recognized that the Amendment Act had been duly passed but it held that it was required by Art. II of the Constitution to consider the purpose of all legal rules in applying them to particulars and that this requirement applies to the rule of recognition itself when a question is raised about the validity of legislation. The opinion also stated that Art. II necessarily created an inherent power of judicial review for the decision whether a particular enactment is 'law' requires the application of the rule of recognition in light of its own purposes: to identify as 'laws' the laws of the people of Mythaca made through an Assembly in which they are equally represented. It recognized that there was an implicit rule in the Constitution that the legislature should have the final word on the question whether it has overstepped its authority. But the purpose of this rule, to give effect to the will of the people of Mythaca through its Assembly, could not be disregarded either. The Court indicated that it must weigh these purposes, and interpret the rules accordingly. This was relatively easy for both purposes ran in the same direction, to give effect to the will of the people. The rule of legislative supremacy could not then be invoked to defeat this purpose. The Court also indicated that it may be required to reach a similar decision in other cases involving enactments which are destructive of the fundamental purposes of the Constitution. In such cases, the Court said, it would have to weigh the purposes of the rule of recognition and those of other fundamental rules of the Constitution.

This example indicates how enactments may fail to become law without reference to 'morality' while complying with the prima facie requirements of the rule of recognition. It also exposes the inadequacy of the dichotomy presented by Hart, indicating that at least one additional approach exists which does not conflict with either the positions of legal positivism or of natural law doctrines.

Morality is, therefore, not directly relevant here. The rationality of purposive interpretation is logically quite neutral as to the contents of the rules and the nature of their purposes. It merely requires that interpretation be integrated with, rather than truncated from, the body of purposes it is supposed to serve. The rationality of this kind of interpretation is largely a matter of its consistency.

But, and this is a big 'but', it seems that the effects of this theory *in practice* would be far from neutral with respect to human justice and morality. For there nowadays is a universal practice of incorporating moral ends and purposes into formal constitutional texts and declarations of a legal nature. Perseverance by the judiciary in giving effect to immoral ends (immoral by our lights) is required in the name of consistency only when such ends are openly espoused and proclaimed in the basic constitutional texts of a state. Conversely, where the proclaimed aims and purposes of the constitution reflect our moral inclinations, the same requirement of consistency demands that judges persevere in upholding such ends and purposes in the face of piecemeal enactments designed to promote policies which are irreconcilable with those embedded in the fundamental constitutional arrangements. This theory of interpretation, which we may call the *integral* theory for its demand that the interpretation of laws be consistent with the policies of legal rules, necessarily resists the introduction into a legal system of legislation designed to subvert and override the basic policies of the system. Now it is a fact of political life that the constitutions of even the most detestable regimes, such as those of Mississippi and South Africa, endorse ideals and ends which are surprisingly in harmony with those of the American Constitution. It is equally a fact of political life that there simply are no legal systems which openly promote inequality and privilege and which are openly dedicated to enslave and disregard the rights of racial or ethnic minorities. On the contrary the 120 odd member states of the United Nations are solemnly committed both in the Charter and in the Universal Declaration of Human Rights to promote purposes and policies which have been received with a surprising degree of global unanimity. The formal devotion of even the most repressive regimes to purposes and ideals which they invariably deny to their people is relevant to a theory of interpretation which demands that judges and other state officials give effect only to such laws which are compatible with the purposes and ends solemnly adhered to and proclaimed by their own states. This doctrine would expose the fallacy of a brand of legal positivism which justifies the supine judicial surrender to totalitarian or racist legislation in states in which constitutional arrangements and solemn declarations of purpose uphold the universally recognized principles of human rights. Our theory, in removing the theoretical justification for judicial compliance with legislative enormities, would fasten full personal responsibility on judges and other state officials who are prepared to enforce such legislation in clear disregard of the ends and ideals publicly espoused by their legal system. It would expose such action as judicially unwarranted collaboration with repressive measures.

The integral theory of interpretation would no doubt put the judiciary of totalitarian states in an unenviable dilemma. It invites them to resist legislation which violates the fundamental tenets of the public theory of their regimes. It would leave no recourse for such states but to embark on a course of flagrant illegality and compel them to openly change their constitutional arrangements, thus weakening the legitimacy of their repression. These, of course, are matters better considered by the political scientist. But they would suggest an answer to Hart's question about the practical merits of a narrower concept of law. The paradigm of the Nazi regime which is generally introduced in this context may not be that useful. The regimes contending for the mantle of Hitlerism are neither as extreme nor as impervious to pressure. They operate their nefarious apparatus behind the facade of commitments to contemporary universal ideals, so as to retain legitimacy at home and respectability abroad. A doctrine for the critical appraisal of repugnant enactments may well make judges readier to desregard the will of unrepresentative legislatures. Another merit of the narrower view of law would be to extract, at least in theory, the state machinery of law enforcement from the disrepute in which it has been plunged by a theory which requires judicial deference to the superior will of the most oppressive legislators.

These practical considerations would not by themselves justify a theory of interpretation. Indeed there is a healthy puritan instinct to distrust theories which serve one's purpose too well, but surely this puritanism cannot be pushed to the point of disqualifying a theory on this ground alone. This theory does not, however, suggest that the certification of an enactment as legally valid is conclusive of the question of the *moral* duty to obey it. Morally iniquitous rules may still be law, and the necessity for individual moral judgments on the question of obedience to such laws is not by any means avoided.

The definition of law

These remarks situate the meaningful context of the problem of the definition of law. The problem of demarcation between legal, moral and other rules is, as we suggested, a practical one arising in the process of the application of law. It is an untypical problem for in the vast majority of cases no questions are raised about the legal validity of the rules invoked before courts and other official organs. However, when such questions are raised they can be disposed of by reference to the rule or rules of reconigtion. This rule is thus used generally in cases of a marginal character, and these cases are resolved by its *application*. In other words, the line of demarcation between legal and non-legal rules is established from time to time by *decisions* which are themselves governed by the accepted rule of recognition, and as we have emphasized, such applications of a rule of recognition like the application of all rules involves the consideration of purposes. A legal rule can, therefore, be defined as a rule which is recognized to be a legal rule pursuant to the application of a rule of recognition. Thus while the question 'is this statement a rule?' can be answered by reference to its practical ability to guide inferences in a certain manner, the question 'is this a *legal* rule?' cannot be answered by reference to such ability to guide but involves also a *legal judgment*. The first question 'is this a rule?' involves therefore the ascertainment of some *functional* characteristics of the statement about which it arises. It can be answered in almost factual terms, 'yes, it is designed to and can be used to guide inferences of a certain kind'. The second question, 'is this a *legal* rule?' involves however the *application* of rules of recognition, it cannot be answered in factual terms. Thus while the form of the two questions is very similar, they require in effect totally different kinds of answers. The first question does not require a judgment of policy, the second does

– it is itself a request for a legal decision rather than for factual information.

For example, at international law a considerable degree of discussion sometimes accompanies the question of demarcation between legal and non-legal rules. At its 20th Session, the General Assembly of the United Nations adopted by a nearly unanimous vote a Declaration on the Inadmissibility of Intervention in the Domestic Affairs of States. Most of the Eastern European and Latin American states asserted that this Declaration was expressive of international law, while the United States and other Western states asserted that it expressed not a legal doctrine but the political consensus of the General Assembly. The appropriate rule of recognition at international law is somewhat involved, (as a matter of fact, as Hart has pointed out, most rules of recognition are composite and it is a matter of convenience that we refer to *the* rule of recognition). Art. 38 of the Statute of the International Court, we pointed out, contains a definition of the law of the Court which applies among other rules, 'international custom, as evidence of a general practice accepted as law' and 'the general principles of law recognized by civilized nations'. The distinction between legal and non-legal rules in this context is somewhat intriguing, for it appears to have little practical significance. A violation of the Declaration by a member state is likely to be followed by the same consequences whether it be considered a legal or a political document. No enforcement machinery was set up to secure its application, and the General Assembly itself – as a political organ – is not likely on the basis of its past record, to draw distinctions between legal and political doctrines if it were to consider the recommendation of enforcement measures.

The import of the distinction, however, may be manifest in a different context. The states which recognize the Declaration as a legal document thus presumably indicate their commitment to abide by it. In the absence of an enforcement machinery they are, however, free to disregard such committment with impunity, and this is what some of them have already done. The states which are unwilling to assign legal significance to the Declaration thus presumably put the other states on notice that they are not committed to give it effect, for the political will of states can be altered at their discretion. In current international practice the two attitudes to the Declaration lead to very similar consequences, for whereas one state will violate international law and its treaty obligations with impunity, another state will abide by the expression of the political will of the community of nations. Another context in which the distinction between legal and non-legal rules may be significant is that of international adjudication. Although the compulsory jurisdiction of the International Court of Justice is limited, it remains a fact that the Court will apply the rules contemplated in Art. 38 of the Statute. The Court would not apply, however, in any controversy before it, rules which are merely hortatory or moral and which have no legal force. It must be noted that in the absence of effective measures for enforcing the Court's judgments under Art. 94 of the Charter, the practical significance of this distinction is reduced, for the decisions of the Court may in practice be given effect only pursuant to the voluntary compliance of the parties. The practical value of the distinction between legal and non-legal rules at international law is, therefore, not as manifest as at municipal law. For the two principal international organs which may be involved in controversies involving such rules, the General Assembly and the Security Council, are political organs, while the judicial organ, the International Court, is not possessed of general compulsory jurisdiction. Moreover, the decisions of these organs cannot be enforced by a judicial or quasi-judicial machinery, and their execution in practice depends upon the voluntary compliance of states with their decisions or recommendations.

This rather technical example from the often mystifying realm of international law indicates that the demarcation between legal rules and other rules may sometimes be neither very meaningful nor very clear. 'Is this law?' is a question that can be most adequately answered when the consequences assigned to the 'legal' character of a rule are well defined and when the rule of recognition is applied and relied upon by the organ concerned with the demarcation between legal and non-legal rules. It is a question which is meaningful in the context of the application of rules to concrete cases.

X

PRINCIPLED CHOICE
AND COMPETING INTERESTS

The doctrine of 'balancing' and its philosophical foundations

The accusation is nowadays commonly heard that the Supreme Court of the U.S. engages in balancing competing interests on a less than wholly principled basis.[1] It raises issues fundamental to the investigation of rule-guided decisions; questions which may surprise readers more familiar with the doctrine of the supremacy of Parliament. It is also quite common, in some schools of jurisprudence, to think of law in terms of a conflict between living policy and felt claims, and between legal rules and precedent.[2] This perilous dichotomy seems to have gained solidity in the disputes associated with an alleged divergence of approach attributed to Harvard and Yale. We indicated earlier that the concept of rule, far from being a static instrument of guidance, is intimately connected with the concepts of purpose and policy. Moreover, we suggested that rules presuppose that the consideration of policy arises at two levels: at the level of legislation and at the level of application.[3] Since it is possible to regard the concepts of purpose and policy as embedded in the concept of rule, the opposition of the one to the other appears both artificial and damaging. For it encourages legal theorists to turn either with excessive deference or with exaggerated indifference to the guiding hand of rule and principle.

The problem of reasoning governed by rules is essentially a problem of guidance, of authority. The very resort to rules for deciding particular cases indicates a determination to be guided by preexisting directives rather than to reach decisions with unfettered discretion. The application of rules to particular fact situations often requires further guidance and it is for the sake of such further *guidance* that the concept of purpose has been introduced in this analysis. For the consideration of purpose guides and limits the *application* of rules. We suggested that the difficulty in using purposes lies in their proliferation. This difficulty has led in turn to the necessity for choosing between competing purposes. But it is quite important to stress that purposes and policies are not directly applied to fact situations *in a system primarily relying on rules*, but rather that they guide the application of rules in such situations. The multiplicity of inference-guidance tools leading to decisions and choices is not merely 'horizontal' but 'vertical' as well. That is, rules and policies are not *alternative* tools for guiding decisions but they are rather *complementary* in the sense that the use of one may require at some stage resort to the other. Moreover, these are by no means the only two modes of guidance. Examples and standards are also capable of being so used. It is quite artificial to assert that the use of these tools is mutually exclusive. On the contrary, they belong to an integrated system of inference-guidance devices which can be jointly utilized so as to obtain specificity of direction while regaining flexibility of application.

The system of guidance-devices using rules as first-instance directives, requires the utilization of yet another component: the ultimate commitment to prefer some purposes over others. This requires elaboration.

Choices between rival sets of purposes and interests can be made either on a principled, consistent basis or on a non-principled, unfettered basis in each case. This is an inescapable *procedural* option with respect to the mode of choice between purposes and interests in systems using rules for guidance. It is, to borrow a phrase from Karl Jaspers, a 'boundary situation'.[4] But it is a second 'boundary situation' which arises only as a consequence of another 'boundary situation': the unavoidable choice between competing purposes, interests and policies. This procedural option is thrust on all users of rules, on all courts that do not merely desire to 'justify' their decisions, but which are also determined to seek guidance for the application of rules and principles. This procedural option profoundly affects the character of a judiciary and the nature of its functions. It has recently been the subject of an impressive and fundamental debate both within and without the Supreme Court of the United States. This is the debate between Mr Justice Black and the majority of the Court on the propriety of the method of 'balancing' interests in First Amendment* cases, which has generated divided and brilliant scholarly contributions.

Since World War II in particular, the Court has been dominated

---

* 'Congress shall make no law respecting an establishment of religion, or prohibiting the free exercise thereof; or abridging the freedom of speech, or of the press; or the right of the people peaceably to assemble, and to petition the government for a redress of grievances.'

by a philosophy of adjudication founded upon the weighing of competing values.[5] This philosophy contemplates the role of the Court in constitutional issues as the exercise of the choice between competing claims and interests and this choice is deemed to rest upon the exercise of practical judgment based upon the factual particularities of each case rather than upon the guidance of rule or principle.[6] The *locus classicus* of the 'balancing' doctrine is Mr Justice Harlan's opinion in *Konigsberg* v. *State Bar of California*,

'On the other hand, general regulatory statutes, not intended to control the content of speech but incidentally limiting its unfettered exercise, have not been regarded as the type of law the First or Fourteenth Amendment forbade Congress or the States to pass, when they have been further justified by subordinating valid government interests, a prerequisite to constitutionality which has *necessarily* involved a weighing of the governmental interests involved. . . . It is in the latter class of cases that this Court has always placed rules compelling disclosure of prior association as an incident of the informed exercise of a valid governmental function . . . *Whenever*, in such a context, these constitutional protections are asserted against the exercise of valid governmental powers a reconciliation must be effected, and *that perforce requires an appropriate weighing of the respective interests* involved . . . With more particular reference to the present context of a state decision as to character qualifications, it is difficult, indeed, to imagine a view of the constitutional protections of speech and association which would automatically and without consideration of the extent of the deterrence of speech and association and of the importance of the state function, exclude all reference to prior speech or association on such issues as character, purpose, credibility, or intent.'[7] (Emphasis added.)

It is not clear whether the balancing test is meant to be one of general application in all First Amendment issues but it must be noted that Mr Justice Brennan for one, has indicated that it has not been given an across-the-board application in First Amendment cases.[8] Other tests have also been used by the Court and each but for the minority 'absolute' view, has been utilized to sustain government regulation in particular contexts: the 'redeeming social value' test in obscenity cases; the 'clear and present danger' test in regulation of subversive activities and of the publication of matter thought to obstruct justice, and the 'balancing test' primarily in the case of regulations not intended directly to affect the content of speech but incidentally limiting its exercise.[9]

While Mr Justice Brennan is evidently accurate as to the respective areas of application of each test, it appears nevertheless that they have all been administered by the Court, in recent times at least, in a manner that involves some degree of balancing. Thus, the 'redeeming social value' test has been aptly described by Mr Justice Black as '. . . even more uncertain, then is the unknown substance of the Milky Way', *Ginzburg* v. *United States*.[10] It requires a case-by-case assessment of social values by individual judges and jurors. It involves questions upon which no uniform agreement could possibly be reached among groups of any kind. It presupposes, therefore, *ad hoc* appraisals of social value to determine whether a particular material is 'utterly without redeeming social value'.

The 'clear and present danger' test, particularly after the Court's acceptance of Learned Hand's 'restatement', in *Dennis* v. *United States*,[11] has become indistinguishable from the balancing test,

'In each case [courts] must ask whether the gravity of the "evil", discounted by its improbability, justifies such invasion of free speech as is necessary to avoid the danger.'

Paul Freund aptly commented that,

'No matter how rapidly we utter the phrase "clear and present danger", or how closely we hyphenate the words, they are not a substitute for the weighing of values. They tend to convey a delusion of certainty when what is most certain is the complexity of the strands in the web of freedom that the judge must disentangle.'[12]

The balancing approach seems, therefore, to pervade the court's adjudication in the whole area of First Amendment situations even when the court resorts to the 'clear and present danger' and 'redeeming social value' tests.

The balancing approach of the majority of the Court has been under severe criticism, most notably from Mr Justice Black and this criticism goes to the very root of the Court's adjudicative functions. This criticism must not be confused with Mr Justice Black's own theory of 'absolutes'. The objections to the balancing approach are many: (1) it makes constitutional law a series of individual adjudications which cannot be relied upon in later cases and it does not permit the establishment of general principles; (2) judges are not equipped to do an adequate balancing job since they would need to know much more about the probable consequences of proposed decisions; (3) balancing is done without reference to any objective scale or standard and tends to reflect present day needs and views subjectively held by the judges themselves;[13] (4) as applied to date, the test does not really give a chance to the private interests involved, and gives almost conclusive weight to the legislative judgment. For the court will not question the decision of the legislature unless that determination is outside the pale of fair judgment; (5) the test cannot give individuals and state officials advance notice of what the law is. This is a particularly serious matter in criminal cases like the *Ginzburg* case, for in the words of Mr Justice Black, 'the government . . . should not be vested with power and discretion to define and punish as criminal past conduct which had not been clearly defined as crime in advance'.[14] This failure has been listed by Lon Fuller as one of the basic ways to fail to make law;[15] (6) the test disregards, in First Amendment cases, the view advocated by Dr Meiklejohn that under the Constitution the people created a form of government under which they granted only *some* powers to the Federal and State instruments they established and that they reserved to themselves powers of governing importance which are accordingly immune from regulation.[16]

Mr Justice Black's reluctance to allow judges to evaluate competing interests was confirmed by his observation that judges could not be trusted to properly recognize the nature of these interests.[17] He thus echoed the warning of Roscoe Pound that,

'When it comes to weighing or valuing claims or demands with respect to other claims or demands, we must be careful to compare them on the same plane. If we put one as an individual interest and the other as a social interest, we may decide the question in advance in our way of putting it.'[18]

So, in the *Barenblatt* case, Black said that if any weighing was proper, it was not Barenblatt's individual right to refrain from revealing Communist affiliations that should be weighed against the social interest, but the,

'. . . interest of the people as a whole in being able to join organizations, advocate causes and make political "mistakes" without later being subjected to governmental penalties for having dared to think for themselves.'[19]

In the analysis of competing interests, it is, therefore, of the utmost significance that the individual and social interests be recognized to be interchangeable, and that they be recognized to be the same interest merely viewed from a different perspective.[20] Failure to allow for this characteristic of interests carries with it the seeds for the reification of the state or of a particular form of economic order as something transcending the forms of individual life in society.

Mr Justice Black also objected in *Konigsberg* that,

'. . . the application of such a [balancing] test is *necessarily* tied to the emphasis particular judges give to competing societal values. Judges, like everyone else, vary tremendously in their choice of values. This is perfectly natural and, indeed, *unavoidable*. But is it natural or unavoidable in this country for the fundamental rights of the people to be dependent upon the different emphasis different judges put upon different values at different times. For those rights, particularly the First Amendments rights involved here, were unequivocally set out by the Founders in our Bill of Rights in the very plainest of language, and they should not be diluted by "tests" that obliterate them whenever particular judges think values they most highly cherish out-weigh the values most highly cherished by the Founders.' (Emphasis added.)[21]

In this opinion Mr Justice Black echoes the words of Bertrand Russell who has made a lifelong attempt to overcome the limitations of moral relativism,

'I am not, myself, satisfied with what I have read or said on the philosophical basis of ethics. I cannot see how to refute the arguments for the subjectivity of ethical values, but I find myself incapable of believing that all that is wrong with wanton cruelty is that I don't like it . . . . when it comes to the philosophy of moral judgments, I am impelled in two opposite directions and remain perplexed. I should deeply rejoice if I could find or be shown a way to resolve this perplexity, but as yet I remain dissatisfied.'[22]

Charles Fried of Harvard has well said that every decision must finally be taken on the managerial, prudential or particularistic judgment of somebody, but that adjudication must proceed on the basis of the role allocated to courts by the Constitution.[23] This role is defined by the rules setting the limits of the respective competence of the courts and Congress. But surely the role assigned to the courts does not merely involve an allocation of competences as between the courts and the other departments. It also involves the determination of the mode of decision which the courts must adopt. This allocation of competence must also direct the courts how to resolve the 'procedural option' we have referred to. This consideration was eloquently expressed by Herbert Wechsler in his celebrated Holmes Lecture,

'The courts have both the title and the duty when a case is properly before them to review the action of the other branches in the light of constitutional provision, even though the action involves value choices, as invariably action does. In doing so, however, they are bound to function otherwise then as a naked power organ; they participate as courts of law. This calls for facing how determinations of this kind can be asserted to have any legal quality. The answer, I suggest, inheres primarily in that they are – or are obliged to be – entirely principled.'[24]

The difficulty which many commentators have had with Wechsler's position arises out of his understanding of what constitutes a 'principled decision' rather than with his assertion that a court ought not to function as a naked power organ. Surely, the Constitution and indeed the very institution of a judiciary presuppose that judges decide cases before them in a principled manner, i.e. that they be guided by some 'external consideration' rather than by their own unfettered subjective preferences. A principled decision must be based upon some kind of guidance-device which limits discretion. It 'cannot be so flexible as to allow for free wheeling discretion'.[25] A principled decision is, therefore, a guided decision – rather than a decision which can be justified by a principle but which is not guided by it. It must, moreover, be consistent with prior decisions, for the notions of principle and rationality are inextricably enmeshed; principle demanding that like cases be treated alike.

The rationality of the allocation of competences between the courts and Congress, contemplated in the Constitution would be jeopardized if courts were free to exercise their competence in any manner they pleased. The judicial power vested in the courts presupposes at the very least that they exercise their judgment judicially, that is, that they look for the guidance of law and principle wherever such guidance can be had. If the balancing approach does suffer from the defects attributed to it by its critics, particularly the lack of objective standards for constitutional judgments, it would indeed be repugnant to the institutional requirements of adjudication, always provided that another approach can cure those defects. Herbert Wechsler's eloquent plea for principled decision-making applies with particular force to the balancing approach which now looms so large in the Court's mode of conducting its affairs, but which regrettably he did not choose to elaborate upon.

The balancing approach does not rest, however, on juridical grounds alone. It is related in spirit to the prevailing doctrine of ethical relativism which essentially holds that discussion ends when we come to the bedrock of differences in preference.[26] This conviction has been stated with characteristic courage and forthrightness by Hans Kelsen,

'. . . the question as to the highest value in the subjective sense of the term can be decided only emotionally, by the feelings or the wishes of the deciding subject. One subject may be led by his emotions to prefer personal freedom; another, social security; one, the welfare of a single individual; the other, the welfare of the whole nation. By no rational consideration can it be proved that the one is right or the other wrong.'[27]

The philosopher Henry Aiken, in discussing moral reasoning in *Reason and Conduct*, came to a position surprisingly close to that of the majority of the Court. He reaffirmed that,

'. . . men may still reasonably disagree and that, upon reflection, they may properly decide differently as to the weights to be attached to the respective claims of liberty, justice, or least suffering without fear of justifiable recrimination or blame on the part of their peers. . . .'[28]

He then wrote, in a spirit consistent with that of Mr Justice Harlan, a brilliant page which I may be excused for citing at some length,

'For it may be said that, when I am involved in a conflict of basic commitments, I must decide between them and that I cannot justifiably renounce them both. Moreover, it is always in order to demand that a man reconsider and that he review both the facts and principles in question in order to make certain that no vital point has been missed. In short, I am always bound to listen to reason, and this means, in part, that the process of moral reconsideration and justification is never finally closed, even when, for the time being, I find that I must provisionally make up my mind. But having reconsidered, then as a rational agent I am free to choose for myself between the conflicting principles and, in so doing, I may claim to have done everything a reasonable man may be required to do in order to reach an impartial and objective decision. And my decision in such a case will be impartial and objective since no one may fairly claim that I have failed to do what any man ought to have done in the same circumstances, even though some men might reasonably have decided differently. . . .

'This means not that we are here appealing to some special faculty of moral intuition but that we are invoking still another regulative procedure which claims government over the process of deliberation itself. It does not tell us in particular what our first-level duties may be; it provides no formula for weighing the respective claims of conflicting obligations. It tells us only that we must take an impartial or general view, that we must consider how others in our predicament have acted, and that we be prepared to review the facts of the case upon demand. It tells us, in short, what steps we must have taken in our process of justification if our choice is to be held free from blame.'[29]

Aiken's eloquent but resigned plea essentially echoes Kelsen's brutal assertion that there comes a point at which one is necessarily bound to choose between conflicting principles and that nothing more can rationally be done to guide such choice. At this point a misunderstanding must be guarded against. There is a necessary distinction between rules, principles, purposes and policies – whether they are objective or relative – and problems arising about the *choice* between such rules, principles, purposes and policies. Theories about the nature of rules, purposes and policies *do not entail* any conclusion about the choice between them. The two issues are separate and must be kept so. The questions which beset courts arise characteristically not about the validity of the competing interests and policies but in connection with the choices between them. Whatever relativist theories may hold about the justification of purposes and interests does not entail a conclusion that it is possible to found choices *between* them only on arbitrary personal preferences. For guidance may be available for the preferment of some purposes and interests over others. With this in mind, it is instructive to recall Sartre's assertion that man is 'condemned to be free', that he is bound to exercise his choice without the guidance of anything but his conscience.[30] On this point, agreement stretches across philosophical schools; from existentialism to linguistic analysis. Sartre's position is in this respect not far from that of Wittgenstein,

' "How am I able to obey a rule?" – if this is not a question about causes, then it is about the justification for my following the rule in the way I do.

'If I have exhausted the justifications I have reached bedrock, and my spade is turned. Then I am inclined to say: "This is simply what I do." '[31]

The pervasiveness of this viewpoint in the West is now such that it can properly be considered as *the* dominant philosophical attitude, Christian Thomistic and irrationalist theories excepted. It is not then really surprising that M. P. Golding, a professional philosopher, should have reacted with near incredulity to Wechsler's demand for reason and principle in the judicial appraisal of conflicting values,

'I fail to grasp Professor Wechsler's position if it consists in the statement that one ought to, or even can, supply "neutral principles" for "choosing" between competing values. I can, of course, choose between two competing values by reference to a third value which is more comprehensive or supreme, that is, when there is already an order of values. Assuming such an ordering it seems to make sense to speak of "reasoned choice between competing values". Although I doubt it, perhaps this is precisely what Professor Wechsler is implying in his comment on the "preferred position" controversy when he says that it has virtue "insofar as it recognizes that some ordering of social values is essential; that all cannot be given equal weight, if the Bill of Rights is to be maintained". But it is difficult to see how the ordering itself is to be made on "neutral principles".'[32]

It must be surprising and even alarming for lawyers to entertain the thought that courts are influenced in their mode of work by philosophical doctrines fashioned out of the insubstantial web of academic ratiocinations. It may be true, although it is hopefully improbable, that judges never read philosophy, but surely the critique levelled by Mr Justice Black at Mr Justice Harlan that the balancing approach is *necessarily* tied to the subjective preferences of judges is a philosophical statement of sorts, and a statement which is in harmony with modern theories of moral reasoning.

This feature of the balancing doctrine, which Mr Justice Black castigates is, however, also the very reason for its appeal. Under the prevailing theory judges cannot avoid – in issues involving choices between competing interests – making their judgments subjectively since differences in judgment rest on fundamental and perhaps ineradicable differences in preference. The balancing approach would then outline the only proper judicial mode of behaviour: if judges necessarily make choices between competing interests subjectively, it is only fitting that they exercise the utmost restraint in reaching their decisions. The doctrine of judicial restraint then acquires overwhelming weight, for on what grounds can judges in a democracy substitute their own value judgments for those of elected legislators? That such considerations play in the mind of judges is not merely speculation. They are nowhere more apparent than in Judge Learned Hand's lectures on the Bill of Rights,

'We are faced with the ever present problem in all popular government: how far the will of immediate majorities should prevail. Even assuming, as I am, that a suspensive veto would be desirable, then power to annul a statute is much more than that. It does not send back the challenged measure for renewed deliberation; it forbids it by making a *different* appraisal of the values, which, as I have just said, is the essence of legislation. Moreover, judges are seldom content merely to annul the particular solution before them; they do not, indeed they may not, say that taking all things into consideration, the legislators' solution is too strong for the judicial stomach. On the contrary they wrap up their veto in a protective veil of adjectives such as "arbitrary", "artificial", "normal", "reasonable", "inherent", "fundamental", or "essential", whose office usually, though quite innocently, is to disguise what they are doing and impute to it a derivation far more impressive than *their personal preferences, which are all that in fact lie behind the decision.* If we do need a third chamber it should appear for what it is, and not as the interpreter of inscrutable principles.' (Emphasis added.)[33]

Nor is his relativism a secret. He also said in these lectures that,

'If we can find time for some other activity than forging fantastic engines of war and using them to destroy each other, who knows but we shall acquire so intimate an acquaintance with ourselves that we shall indeed discover principles that will be as objectively valid as those that govern inanimate things;'[34]

In such a climate of opinion, when it is asserted that all choices between policies, values, interests and purposes ultimately rest upon the naked preference of the deciding subject, it is a tribute to the integrity of the Supreme Court that it should have been so reluctant to substitute its own judgment for that of the people's representatives. It is a tribute to the Court, that aware of the flimsy foundation of its decisions in issues involving the balancing of interests – in most constitutional issues that is – it should refuse to lay down principles and presume to fetter the future discretion of other judges. For while law, rules and principles are properly laid down for the direction of other judges when preexisting authority to that effect is available, it would be a gross abuse of authority for a court to legislate into binding law the ephemeral value-judgments of the justices of the time and place. The faults attributed to the balancing approach would from such viewpoint, become its very merits.

We see that the prevailing philosophical doubts about the possibility of objective justification of choices between competing policies and interests may have inhibited the exercise of judicial power. This becomes apparent in a characteristic opinion of Mr Justice Frankfurter,

'. . . how are competing interests to be assessed? Since they are not subject to quantitative ascertainment, . . . who is to make the adjustment? – who is to balance the relevant factors and ascertain which interest is in the circumstances to prevail? Full responsibility for the choice cannot be given to the courts. Courts are not representative bodies. They are not designed to be a good reflex of a democratic society. Their judgment is best informed, and therefore most dependable within narrow limits . . .

'Primary responsibility for adjusting the interests which compete in the situation before us of necessity belong to the Congress. . . . We are to set aside the judgment of those whose duty it is to legislate only if there is no reasonable basis for it.'[35]

As Dean Griswold remarked, the great lesson taught by Mr Justice Frankfurter was that the integrity of the judicial process requires a deep awareness on the part of the judge of the limitations of his own powers of decision and of the necessity of seeking to avoid decision on grounds of personal belief.[36] It was indeed a heroic matter for the Court to deny itself powers of review in the face of the quasi-totalitarian legislation of the McCarthy era, but, it must be admitted, it was an effort that nearly led to the wrecking of the treasured liberties which had been enshrined in the Bill of Rights at a time when men did believe in a 'higher law'.

The Supreme Court is thus torn between the conflicting requirements that its appraisal of competing values and interests be principled and based upon reason, a requirement which cannot be met according to some contemporary philosophical traditions, and between the requirement that it refrains from turning into law the shifting value preferences of the transient court majorities substituting their private preferences for those of elected legislators. Viewed in this perspective the critical question for constitutional adjudication is whether courts have the possibility to avoid this dilemma; whether they can avoid deciding issues involving conflicting values otherwise than on the basis of subjective personal preferences, on some sort of principled basis. In other words, is the dichotomy of 'balancing' versus 'principled' decision-making inescapable?

'Balancing' v. 'Absolutes': some other alternatives

The most significant attempt to overcome the limitations of unprincipled decision-making which has so far characterized the balancing test, is the doctrine of 'absolutes'. This doctrine was said to be a call that judges render their decisions concerning the Bill of Rights 'not by using an *ad hoc* balance, but by reference to an underlying balance established by the Constitution'.[37] Under this doctrine, the Constitution is a source of law in the very broadest sense and the doctrine itself is indeed an expression of the search for the rule of law.[38] By that is meant that the Constitution is not regarded merely as a compendium of legal rules to be applied like ordinary statutes; nor is it only an amalgam of variegated principles each designed to promote separate and often conflicting ends. Under this theory, the Constitution is used also as an authoritative guide for choices *between* conflicting interests and values. This does indeed make it different from ordinary statutory legislation where each measure is but an isolated thrust in a given direction adopted often without particular regard for what other statutes and principles are intended to achieve. A statute is enacted with a view to application in light of what it is designed to promote and with the expectation that courts will adjust the boundaries of adjacent policies and purposes. A statute does not generally require courts to disregard the values and policies which it may interfere with in the course of application. Statutes contemplate that courts shall resolve the clashes between purposes and policies and that courts shall decide which shall give way in each case. But it can be otherwise with the Constitution. For the concern of the Founders was to strike a lasting balance between the rights of the individual and those of the community, a balance capable of serving as a guide to courts called upon to decide issues involving similar conflicts of values.[39] This is how Mr Justice Black stated the matter,

'Of course the decision to provide a constitutional safeguard for a particular right, such as the fair trial requirements of the Fifth and Sixth Amendments and the right of free speech protection of the First, involves a balancing of conflicting interest. Strict procedures may release guilty men; protecting speech and press may involve dangers to a particular government. I believe, however, that the Framers themselves did this balancing when they wrote the Constitution and the Bill of Rights. They appreciated the risks involved and they decided that certain rights should be guaranteed regardless of these risks. Courts have neither the right nor the power to review this original decision of the Framers and to attempt to make a different evaluation of the importance of the rights granted in the Constitution. Where conflicting values exist in the field of individual liberties protected by the Constitution, that document settles the conflict and policy should not be changed without constitutional amendments by the people in the manner provided by the people.'[40]

It is easy indeed to misrepresent this doctrine – admittedly the tag of 'absolute' is somewhat unfortunate. But Dr Meiklejohn has rightly chided Mr Justice Harlan for misrepresenting this doctrine.[41] It does not suggest that in First Amendment cases all words, writing and other communications should always be free from all government regulation. Nor does it suggest that the words of the First Amendment can be directly applied to the facts of a case without difficulty. Problems of definition and of application are not solved by waving the wand of absolutes. Nor has this been suggested. Much of the criticism levelled at the doctrine has failed to discriminate between the various roles which the Bill of Rights can be called upon to play. The Bill of Rights can thus be used like any other body of rules which directly governs factual issues; it is not then exempt from the difficulties of definition and meaning characteristic of all applications of rules to fact situations. Its role, however, does not end there. It can also play another, different part, and be taken to have established an underlying balance, a commitment intended to endure as long as the Constitution itself. This commitment, *to prefer* the individual rights safeguarded by the Bill of Rights over the claims and interests of government, is operative on a level entirely different from that of governing rules. It is operative as a guide to the resolution of choices of value which arise in connection with the application of rules; it cannot then be applied to facts directly, it can merely guide the application of rules and the choices between interests and values which such application requires.

This distinction has some implications which were overlooked by the critics of the absolute theory. The use of the Bill of Rights as a source of preferred values, does not require that refinement of meaning and preciseness of definition which is required when rules are directly applied to specific factual occurrences The choice between values and interests can then be indicated in simple language which can be read quite literally. The failure of the literal theory of meaning arose, we must remember, in a very different context. It arose when words had to be applied to particulars, in situations when words are but delegations of the authority to apply them. Nor is such application called for when the Bill of Rights is read with a view to following the balances struck by the Framers. In such circumstances, the 'ordinary meaning' of words suffices to express the preference for some values at the expense of others, their application is then no longer to specifics. The Bill of Rights then functions as an exemplary resolution of irreconcilable claims and principles. Nor can it as such become 'dated' or 'obsolete'. For it is a source not only of rules – and these may require change even though their objectives remain constant – but also of a commitment to a particular kind of society. The options presented to the Framers have not markedly changed and are not likely to be metamorphosed even though the instrumentalities nowadays threatening their cherished values evolve as do all technologies. In moral theory as in political philosophy there is little change in the options open to man in society; change occurs only in the instrumentalities for the accomplishment of preferred goals. Commitment is, therefore, immune to changing circumstances, novel technologies and heinous enemies. This is the sense in which Mr Justice Black, the 'backward country fellow' has read the Bill of Rights, again displaying his extraordinary sensibility and perception of what it is to expound a Constitution.

The balancing theory, on the other hand, by attaching weight to the consequences of particular decisions has obscured in yet another way the true subjectivity of its own standards.[41a] These consequences and facts are not endowed with any intrinsic value. It is the very choice between consequences which sets the standards in each case. The pretence that consequences require a decision conceals the truth that it is the very choice or preference that sets the values. No amount of investigation or reasoning about the factual circumstances of any particular case can extract a principle for the resolution of conflicts of interests inherent in the application of rival legal rules to those particular facts. In other words, investigation of the material facts of a case will tell us nothing about the applicable rules or preferred values. Investigation of an occurrence is logically distinct from investigation of guidance-devices. Refined investigation of the facts may disclose the applicability of a wider variety of legal rules and principles than suspected. Yet it can tell nothing about the *choice between* rules and principles. The choice between them turns on considerations that are distinct from anything which the facts of the case can disclose. The *ad hoc* balancing of interests cannot, therefore, be justified by the pseudo-pragmatic emphasis on facts. It rests on the fallacy that the facts of a case and the rules and interests involved are all 'facts' of a similar nature. And such a fallacy provides a semblance of rationality to what really is but an instance of un-principled decision-making.

The doctrine of absolutes, on the other hand, manages to give practical guidance to courts and officials concerned with the application of rules. It thereby furnishes a principled source of decision-making, without, at the same time, elevating subjective judicial preferences into law or principle. It can be objected that the Bill of Rights was not intended by the Framers as a once-and-for-all resolution of the contest between values and interests. Whatever the accuracy of this objection happens to be, it really is beside the point. For what matters is the institutional requirement that judges find authority and guidance for decisions involving such conflicts. In this search for authority, courts may legitimately seize upon indications of exemplary choices between values in acts of national commitment: the Constitution is the principal but by no means the exclusive source of authoritative balancing to which courts ought to be faithful. Courts may properly look also to other documents publicly proclaimed which incorporate solemn declarations of intent such as the Universal Declaration of the Rights of Man and the purposes and principles of the United Nations Charter. These documents, no less than the Bill of Rights, are designed to indicate that states which adhere to them are bound to abide by the preferences articulated by their framers and that courts have neither the right nor the power to review the commitments so adopted nor to make a different evaluation of the importance of the values preferred.

The search for the rule of law has thus been understood by Justices Black and Douglas not merely as the search for legal rules and legislative policies, but also as the quest for preferred values and interests.[42] It is somewhat odd that Mr Justice Frankfurter who was so concerned not to displace the value preferences of Congress by the Court's own subjective judgments, did not adopt the one mode of decision which would have enabled the Court to fetter its own discretion, i.e. adherence to the balances struck by the Framers. He failed to explain how courts can afford to ignore the value commitments of the Framers and to reconcile this position with the very principles which compel in his mind deference to the value preferences of Congress. Surely, he somewhat simplified the issue when he presented constitutional questions involving First Amendment cases as a contest between Congressional and judicial judgment, for he left out the third major participant in such a contest, the judgment of the Framers as to preferred values.

The 'absoluteness' of the guarantees of individual rights in the Constitution refers not to the exercise of these rights but to their preferment over other claims. What is absolute, hence unalterable, is the *balancing* done by the Framers, and not, for example, the license to speak.

This now requires qualifications which look regrettably like sophistry. They are nevertheless genuinely inescapable. Were it asserted that the balancing between competing values and interests is absolute not merely in the sense of being unalterable but also in the sense of the preferment of one value to the exclusion of all others, the doctrine could easily lead to untoward results. But this is not, we submit, its true meaning. The doctrine requires that the interests authoritatively preferred by the Framers be consistently respected by the courts. This does not require the dismissal of conflicting interests. For example, under the absolute view, the interest in the safeguard of internal order by government regulation has been subordinated by the Framers to the interest in the safeguard of the freedom of speech. This does not mean that in applying *governing* rules internal order is always to give way to free speech. Let us consider a situation in which speech (rather than conduct) presents an overwhelming and immediate threat to internal order. The preferment of speech (rather than the erection of free speech as the only supreme value) may not then require that the legal rules designed to promote freedom of speech be given effect if the consequence would be the overwhelming, immediate and complete collapse of internal order. In other words, *it is quite consistent to prefer a certain value over another, and yet in 'extreme circumstances' to disregard a legal rule designed to promote it.* 'Extreme' that is with respect to the overwhelming impact which failure to disregard the rule would have on a less favoured value, which although less favoured, is nonetheless not entirely disregarded. This analysis smacks of the return to an invigorated 'clear and present danger' test, free of Judge Learned Hand's gloss. But the preferment of freedom of speech in the Bill of Rights is such that it would tax the imagination to conceive of any speech, as distinct from conduct, which could lead to such an overwhelming and immediate threat to internal security as to warrant regulation.

This 'overwhelming and immediate prospect of chaos' test does indeed lead back to a variety of balancing. Sidney Hook recently remarked that in balancing it is not necessary to give equal weight to the claims and values balanced. He also argued that there can be such a thing as balancing guided by preferred values. Although Sidney Hook severely criticized the doctrine of absolutes he would no doubt recognize the cogency of preferred balancing and of the doctrine of absolutes *if* that is what it means. As Robert McKay has observed, it is indeed the feature of preferredness which is at stake.[43] Moreover, it seems not to have been seriously challenged by anyone on the Supreme Court before Justices Frankfurter and Harlan. Preferredness involves an element of guidance and principle which can remove the decision from the unfettered discretion of the deciding judge. Preferredness therefore does more for a decision than indicate that one value is prima-facie valid over other apparently justified claims in situations of conflict. It also provides a fount of principle and authority which the *ad hoc* balancing of values assigned equal weight denies. Sidney Hook who

took Justices Black and Douglas so severely to task had little sym-
pathy for balancing in which all elements are assigned equal weight.
He cited an example from moral reasoning,

'How is it with ordinary moral reasoning? Can any moral imperatives be more categorical than those which enjoin us against lying,
stealing, or abandoning the helpless? When we balance other
interests – even other moral interests – against them, do we start
from scratch and with nice impartiality equate all competing
interests? This would be to exhibit moral cretinism, a sign that a
thinking machine had run amok.'[44]

In questions of *moral* choice, the final authority for guidance and
decision on the preferment of values is not always compelling; it
may have to be one's own conscience. Moreover, the values themselves may not seem to matter much if we are free to choose them.
This second objection has been met with Sartre's answer,

'. . . I am very sorry that it is so; but if I have done away with God
the Father, there must then be someone to invent values. One must
accept things as they are. And by the way, to say that we invent
values merely means this: life has no a priori meaning. Before you
are alive, life itself is nothing, and it is up to you to give it meaning,
and value is nothing but the meaning that you choose.'[45]

When judicial reasoning is committed to follow all available
authority and guidance it is not faced with the awesome task of
constituting its own values. This is the task of the Founders, of the
Framers, not the task of judges. When there is readiness to act upon
someone else's balancing, much of the anxiety and the agony of
decision is removed. In reasoning guided by rules there is therefore
a way of being principled without legislating one's own preferences
into law. This is what the dissenters on the Supreme Court have
taught us.

It must be admitted, however, that there may arise clashes of
interests and values which cannot be resolved by preexisting
balances and preferments for the simple reason that none exist. It is
then up to the courts to define their role and to decide what to do
when they are unrelentedly confronted with such irreducible conflicts. The dilemma is then hard indeed. Mr Justice Frankfurter's
philosophy – that the proper role of courts is to defer to Congressional judgment when they are confronted with a fair exercise of

such judgment – is then more persuasive. For principled decision-making, when no inference-guidance devices are available to govern policy choices, may well consist in non-interference with the will of the legislator. The allocation of competences contemplated by the Constitution between the Congress and the courts should be seen in the broader context of the allocation of competences between the Framers and Congress. The demands of principled decision-making for the choice between competing values may thus require consistent deference to the value choices of another department. But the same demands require deference, above all, to the choices of value of the authors of the Constitution, the Bill of Rights and the other Declarations of principle and purpose which are incorporated into the law of the land under the Supremacy Clause.

It would appear, in conclusion, that much of the disagreement in the Supreme Court over the application of the First Amendment stems from a failure by the majority to recognize that the Court could turn to the Amendment not merely as a source of governing rules designed to promote freedom of speech and religion. It could turn to it *also* as a source of authoritative balancing between the competing claims of the state and individuals in the area of free speech. For preferred values no less than specific rules, are 'law' in the sense that they can and ought to guide judicial reasoning and determine the application of technical rules. The majority failed also to recognize that under the Constitution courts are bound to abide by the choice between competing interests which were made by the Framers; the majority was so preoccupied by the problem of deference to Congressional will that in the process it lost sight of the problem of deference to the Framers' will. As a result, in the use it made of the balancing test, notably in the *Konigsberg* case, it arrogated to itself a degree of discretion greater than it would have needed pursuant to Mr Justice Black's demand that it give effect to the preferences enshrined in the Bill of Rights. Of all tests used by the court, the *ad hoc* balancing test as administered by Mr Justice Harlan fails most clearly to meet the demands of principled decision-making. These demands are more strictly respected in the other principal approaches to the judicial task which have been evident in the work of the Supreme Court: (1) the technique of balancing when a preferred status is given to First Amendment rights; (2) the absolute test when it is interpreted as deference to the balancing done by the Framers; (3) the doctrine that the people did not vest the authority to regulate speech in the Federal or state instruments of government they had created, and that no balancing could create such authority; (4) the doctrine that the courts should defer to the choices of value made by Congress unless these are made without any 'reasonable' basis.

These doctrines emphasize the importance of principle and authority in decision-making. They underscore the importance of guidance for decision and of direction for the application of rules. They must, however, be carefully set apart from doctrines emphasizing the importance of the justification of judgments. We have repeatedly suggested that some types of rules and principles of justification cannot be used to *guide* decisions and judgments particularly when alternative opposing sets of such rules can be relied upon with equal ease. For the outcome of a judgment then turns on the choice of the appropriate rule or principle of justification. The obverse is not true, for when a rule or principle of guidance is legitimate, when it is proper to rely upon it for directing a decision, then that very rule can also be cited in justification. The two operations, the guidance of a decision or judgment by rule or principle and its justification, are quite distinct. We have already referred to Karl Llewellyn's suggestion in *The Common Law Tradition* that the common law case method relying on competing techniques for the use of precedent uses these techniques to *justify* decision and puts far less stress on the choice between policies and interests. These are really two separate uses which can be made of rules. Our concern here lies primarily with the guidance and direction of judicial reasoning rather than with its *ex post facto* justification, so that examples derived from the method used by the United States Supreme Court are often more germane than those provided by kindred House of Lords decisions. Principled decision-making in a system which requires that decisions be merely *justified* by reference to rules is an easy matter especially when stores of accepted techniques for the use of precedents and statutes are readily available. Such a system provides an aura of neutrality and detachment which is frequently missed in systems requiring that decisions be reached in reliance upon preexisting and independent authority. In systems of reasoning which utilize rules, the policies are often those of separate agencies. Separate that is with regard to the persons making and applying them. It is only fitting that in such systems the governing preferences of policies and purposes should also be separate. This is precisely what makes for the possibility of fairness and impartiality.

Rationality: a postscript

The concept of rationality which has been progressively developed in the course of this work cannot be reduced to three or four components. We have already outlined some of the demands of rationality in an earlier chapter and it is now incumbent on us to concentrate on some other recurrent features.

We have seen that rationality may involve not only the guidance of reasoning but also its justification, and that while both sets of mental operations have different functions, they may nevertheless be resorted to concurrently and are indeed so used in legal arguments in which justificatory procedures play a key role. Guidance of mental operations by inference-guidance devices imposes its own complex demands. These are primarily the demands of aptness for purpose, for all inference-guidance devices are designed to govern mental operations with an end-in-view. Consequently the concept of purpose is intimately involved in all such operations. The proper use of rules as guidance devices requires, in many cases, a model *sequence* of mental operations, only the first set of which is guided by rules. The subsequent sequences rely on purposes and on preferred policies or commitments. Since the use of rules requires a sequence of mental operations which depends upon other forms of guidance, it would seem that rationality involves the complementary use of integrated inference-guidance devices.[46a] A system of rules like a legal system cannot be adequately used without reference to the concepts of purpose, policy and the notion of preferred interests. Moreover, the concept of consistency is intimately connected with the concept of rule with which it bears a close 'family resemblance'.[46]

Yet, a consistent sequence of guided mental operations is not all that rationality demands, for points arise at which guidance dries up. Guidance and necessity are mutually exclusive, for what *must* be, is obviously unavoidable. Necessity in the use of rules often arises in the form of unavoidable options, of choices from which there is no escape. In a sense of course, such necessity has some affinity with guidance for it is absolutely compelling. The options which must be resolved impose choices which are characteristically the last mental step in reasoning involving the use of rules. These necessary options relate both to existential alternatives (i.e. one must be either alive or dead) and to conceptual dilemmas (i.e. the use of rational or non-rational procedures). Such inescapable options and dilemmas are precisely the point at which guidance for mental operations stops ('guidance' which must be distinguished from mere argument). They represent the terminal point of the sequences of authoritative reasons. But though inescapable choices and dilemmas are the boundary at which rationality ends, it is fallacious to infer that what lies beyond that line is irrational; it is rather extra-rational or non-rational. The rational position requires that reliance be placed on inference-guidance devices only so long as such devices are available. When there simply are none to guide, necessity excludes the possibility of reliance. It is fallacious to describe the resolution of options made in such circumstances as irrational, for what is unavoidable cannot be irrational.

Karl Popper's plea that choices, commitments, guidance devices and their applications be held open to criticism has been only recently fully articulated and it already forms an inseparable component of the rationalist position. Criticism, however, must itself be rational, based upon the demands of consistency, necessity, or empirical evidence. The possibility to give grounds for the criticism of a sequence of reasoning does not do away with the need for guidance-devices on which such reasoning can rely. Both procedures, each in their own way, narrow the mesh of rationality refining and sharpening argument.

In a sense, of course, reasoning guided by rules is the most fundamental form of reasoning, for as we indicated earlier the use of language itself may involve a species of rule-guided mental operations. Knowledge, modes of being and of speech are all proper ends for such rule-governed operations. The use of legal rules, which pre-empted the stage of our argument, merely illuminates some of the problems common to all forms of reasoning with rules. The four main sequences of mental operations involving the use of rules – identification of the material facts, application of the rule to facts, consideration of the policy of relevant rules and the preferment of some policies over others – are inherent, it would seem, in rule-guided systems of reasoning generally. The forging and criticism of consistent sets of devices for guiding mental operations and their enlightened use lies therefore at the heart of rationality.

XI

CONCLUSION

The positions developed in this book invite attack on a variety of fronts. The model of rule-directed inferences introduces a formal structure for arguments which is far removed from the familiar logic of the sciences and deductive logic. It rests primarily upon the concept of rule which has been clarified in this analysis. Let us review some implications.

(i) The 'internal' and 'external' aspects of rules are not exhaustive

According to this inquiry what a rule characteristically does is not primarily to describe behaviour – it cannot be assimilated to observable patterns of conduct – nor does it primarily account for the manner in which members of a group who accept it view their own regular behaviour. This concept of rule does not therefore fit into Hart's dichotomous consideration of the 'internal' and 'external' aspect of rules.

The concept of rule has undergone sea changes in recent analysis. It is related, as we have seen, to the concepts of norm, command, prescription and imperatives. R. M. Hare views all norms as species of prescriptive language. Von Wright points out that norm-formulations linguistically speaking are a varied lot. His analysis of norms leads him to the well-known 'classical theory of the nature of norms'. This is the will-theory of norms according to which norms are the expressions or manifestations of the will of some norm-authority with regard to the conduct of some norm-subject. A. Ross writes 'It seems obvious that they [legal rules] must be directives, neither exclamations nor assertions. The law is not written in order to impart theoretical truths, but to direct people – judges and private citizens alike – to act in a certain desired manner.' He adopts the term 'directives' since it is a current specific term for utterances without representative meaning, he finds it more appropriate than 'command' or 'imperative'. Kelsen's influential theory also puts emphasis on prescribed conduct, 'A "norm" is a rule expressing the fact that somebody ought to act in a certain way, without implying that anybody really "wants" the person to act that way.' He thus avoids many of the difficulties involved in viewing law as a 'command', that is, the expression of a will. Kelsen's 'ought' is wholly de-psychologized. The statement that an individual 'ought' to behave in a certain way means in his view that this behaviour is prescribed by a norm. It does not refer to any 'wills' or 'commands'. H. L. A. Hart finds the concept of rule as perplexing as law itself, although he also believes that without the idea of a rule we cannot hope to elucidate even the most elementary forms of law. He distinguishes two aspects of rules: the 'external' point of view which limits itself to the observable regularities of the behaviour of persons following rules, and the 'internal' aspect, which accounts for the manner in which members of a group who accept the rules view their own regular behaviour. The Realists, we may recall, believe that rules are mere tools for the prediction of judicial decisions but their extreme views on the subject have been largely discredited. We should also mention Rawls who distinguishes two concepts of rule. One regards rules as reports that cases of a certain sort have been found on *other* grounds to be properly decided in a certain way. This type of rule involves the justification of a particular action falling under a practice. The other type justifies the practice itself. On this second view rules are pictured as defining a practice and it is essential that it be possible to act upon them.

The concept of rule developed in this book characterizes rules as devices for the guidance of *mental processes* of inference leading to choices, decisions, actions, attitudes, judgments, conclusions and the like. These mental processes must be distinguished from feelings and dispositions for they involve sets of mental operations. In this analysis therefore rules are understood to be tools for guiding *inferences* leading to action rather than directly governing action or conduct.

This way of looking at rules enables us to focus attention on features such as their essential purposiveness, their presupposed contexts of application and the relevance of consequences to their proper use. It is not subjective or psychological in the intendment of Hart's 'internal aspect' of rules. Rules are here regarded as tools of communication for the guidance of some species of mental operations which are not as elusive as verificationist criteria might suggest. For these mental operations which rely upon rules for guidance are, we must remember, recordable events in one sense at least: they can be timed. They are, to use Ryle's helpful formula, clockable occurrences. Rules function on our minds very much like printed letter characters which lead or guide the mental operation of reading. This characterization enables us to disregard the reductionist error of assimilating rules to observable patterns of behaviour and it permits us to explode the dichotomy suggested by Hart's two aspects of rules – their internal and external aspects which are perhaps more helpful in considering the concepts of 'obligation' and 'binding rule'.

This characterization of rules also discloses the need for the differentiation between various forms of inference-guidance devices such as commands, policies and standards which all, in some way, are intended to provide directives for mental processes.

(ii) *Legal rules do not 'exist' in the sense that simple rules do*

While a rule is a communication device which can be said to 'exist' when it is articulated in a form which makes reliance upon it possible, the 'existence' of a legal rule is another matter. Such existence presupposes first its existence as a rule and then also its recognition as a rule which it is the job of the organs of the state to follow and apply. This recognition involves, we have seen, the application of rules of recognition inviting consideration of the purposes and the policies which these rules of recognition are designed to promote. This characterization enables us to conclude that while the existence of a rule is a matter of fact (of sorts) – can it be used as a rule? – the existence of a *legal* rule is not merely a matter of fact but involves in addition a decision which requires the application of yet other rules.

(iii) *Rules v. policy*

Rules are purposive inference-guidance devices. The application of rules thus requires consideration of their purposes. Policy and purpose can obviously also be applied directly without resort to rules. Such use of policy and purpose involves a considerable delegation of authority to those entrusted with execution, it is the hallmark of managerial decision-making. Much of the confusion on the role of policy in the law arises from an alleged rivalry between rule-oriented and policy-oriented decision-making. While obeying rules without consideration of what they are for may be a characteristic demand of hierarchic or military relationships, following or applying rules in a judicial manner involves the consideration both of the rules and of their objects. In hierarchic relationships in which a subordinate is expected to 'obey' a rule, the delegation of authority by the superior is much narrower than in relationships in which the addressee of a rule is expected to consider both its language and function. The execution of policy without reference to rules at all – managerial decision-making – involves an even greater delegation of authority.

All inference-guidance systems involve a varying degree of delegation of authority but none can completely exclude all such delegation. As Professor Dworkin has observed, there is no sharp line between authority and discretion which corresponds to the division between rules and policies. The continuum from authority to discretion is particularly significant in international and in constitutional law where a large measure of discretion is delegated to sovereign states and to the Supreme Court respectively. There is an appreciable variety in the precision of guidance which inference-guidance devices are capable of, and a corresponding degree of delegation of discretion. The more general the guidance or the more obscure, contradictory, or the vaguer it is, the more discretion and freedom it permits in application.

(iv) *Rules of justification v. rules of guidance*

Another distinction has been noticed – that between rules designed to guide and rules designed to justify decisions. Justificatory rules, such as rules of statutory construction and rules for the use of precedent, are unlike rules of guidance in one fundamental respect. Since these rules are frequently conflicting they are generally incapable of providing effective guidance. Reference to such rules in justification does not mean that they were relied upon. They serve rather to legitimize decisions already taken on other grounds. While rules of guidance limit discretion and can always be used in justification, rules of justification which are incapable of providing effective guidance delegate very broad discretion to those destined to use them. For example the discretion of a driver confronted with conflicting one way signs is larger than that of a driver faced with an ordinary such sign. Rules of justification in effect serve to enlarge the freedom of courts to judge cases on policy grounds.

(v) *The connection between legal rules, morality, purposes and interests*

This characterization of rules also underscores the necessary connections between legal rules, morality, purposes and policies. This connection unavoidably arises whenever legal rules are applied or relied upon, for then considerations of purposes, policies and choices between such purposes and policies are inescapable unless one is prepared to disregard what it is that the relevant rules are designed to accomplish; unless, in other words, one is prepared to allow the self-defeating application of rules. This connection permeates the very characterization of a rule as legal. Moreover this characterization underscores the proliferation of purposes and policies relevant to the application of a rule. The aims of certainty and clarity in adjudication can then be restored to their proper proportions and cannot be said to be the *only* policies with claims to govern the application of rules. While the relationship between law-making and morality has not been considered here, it is fairly evident that it plays a very prominent role in the legislative formulation of laws. Thus whether the formulation or the application of legal rules be considered, the impact of extraneous considerations is unavoidable. Moreover, the application of rules to facts always requires a decision involving the selection of material facts based upon more or less overt considerations of purpose and policy.

(vi) *The concept of rule and international law*

The investigation of the concept of rule also has a bearing upon international law. When states in their dealings with each other refer to, or rely upon rules they seldom do so with a view to adjudication. The role of adjudication in the international legal order is nowadays marginal indeed. The rules applied in proceedings before the International Court of Justice which are laid down in Article 38 of the Statute of the Court do not exhaust the categories of rules which states act, rely upon or use in other contexts. Rules are also used by states in their dealings outside the Court, in their diplomatic contacts, in their claims and counter-claims, in regional and in international organizations and of course in the United Nations Organizaion. The large body of rules used and relied upon by states in these contexts includes resolutions of the General Assembly of the U.N. as well as the laws, rules and practices of the principal international organs.

As we have indicated, the *decision* to characterize a rule as legal, involves in a domestic law context its recognition as a rule which it is the job of the organs of the state to follow and apply. The decision to characterize a rule as 'international law' takes place in a totally different context and must serve other purposes, for there is little international compulsory adjudication and even less enforcement of the law. The traditional identification of international legal rules as the rules applied by the International Court of Justice may be too restrictive. It leaves out some rules which states recognize as 'binding' and 'obligatory'. It raises the difficult question whether it makes any sense to consider some rules as 'binding' and yet nevertheless not 'law'. This question is particularly difficult in a field in which even 'law' is not generally enforced but depends in the last resort upon voluntary compliance by states which recognize it as binding. In the absence of adequate enforcement the concept of a 'binding' rule must necessarily be understood in terms of the subjective disposition of states. To say then that an international rule is 'binding' can be understood to mean that there is a commitment voluntarily to comply with it and to recognize claims based upon it. International legal rules in the sense of article 38 of the Statute of the Court are thus binding but some others are equally so. Clearly some of the resolutions of the General Assembly of the U.N. are recognized by states to be fully binding and obligatory. Moreover, it is common knowledge that most of the solemnly ratified treaties, in the event of breach, are not likely to be secured by more effective enforcement than mere resolutions of the General Assembly. These remarks do not touch upon the difficult problem of how 'obligations' can be imposed on third states under international law. It is nevertheless questionable whether it makes sense in international relations to be overtly concerned about the demarcation between international legal rules and other rules in the sense of article 38 of the Statute. It may be more fruitful to concentrate on the rules recognized as 'binding' in the international order.

(vii) *Principled choice between competing values and interests*

Another matter which this analysis involves is the question whether it is possible for a court to choose or balance policies, purposes or values in a principled manner or whether such choices

L

are necessarily subjective and the balance is that of the individual members of the court.

The choice between competing purposes and interests does not arise here in the context of their *direct* application to the facts of a case. These choices arise as a step in the process of reasoning in the application of rules to such facts.

By interests and values we have here referred to congeries of purposes which are promoted by the rules of a system. The choice between rival purposes and interests is inescapable in reasoning with rules when requests for guidance are made after answers have been given in terms of rules, canons of interpretation and the statement of purposes. Such a choice is in the nature of a boundary situation from which there is no escape. It is an inevitable alternative.

Decisions and choices can be guided by a variety of techniques. None of these removes *all* discretion in their application, but all of these remove *complete* discretion. The main techniques for such guidance are:

i. rules, principles,
ii. standards,
iii. purposes, policies,
iv. examples, decided cases,
v. preexisting and binding commitments.

They are moreover not mutually exclusive.

Decisions and choices between purposes and interests can also be taken on an *ad hoc* basis without the help of any preexisting guidance tool.

The question at issue in such choices is whether they should be made on a principled and consistent basis or *ad hoc*, *de novo* in each case.

The option as to the modes of choice between purposes and interests is also a boundary situation from which there is no escape. It is the second boundary situation involved in such choosing. Courts must opt for a particular mode of dealing with such choices and their option will determine the character of their role in adjudication. This determination is separate from the question whether courts ought to reach their decisions on principles transcending the case they are deciding. This latter question refers to the formulation of rules and principles which courts apply to the facts of a situation. The question considered here, on the other hand, refers to the principled choosing between purposes and interests which arise independently of the facts of each case.

The prevailing positivist theories hold that the choices between rival sets of purposes and interests, like between competing values, ultimately rest on personal preferences and that they cannot be justified either by reference to *a priori* norms for these must in turn be justified, nor by reference to factual statements for one cannot derive an 'ought' from an 'is'. This theory has had a strong impact on approaches to adjudication for it suggests that all judicial choices between purposes and interests rest in the final analysis on the personal preferences of the judges involved. In so-called clear cases, judges are bound by rules, but in the more difficult cases they have considerable discretion. This philosophy provides the foundation for the dichotomy of rule v. discretion. Since it suggests that judges cannot reach principled and impartial judgments when they must choose between rival purposes and interests it also suggests that they should be careful not to erect their own judgments and preferences into principle and that the best they can do is to reach individual judgments on the merits of each case.

The prevailing positivist moral philosophy also inspires a theory of judicial review. Since the choice between purposes and interests, like between values, necessarily rests on arbitrary personal preferences, courts should be careful not to substitute their own judgments and choices for those of elected assemblies and officials.

The objections to the implications of positivist moral philosophy for adjudication rest on the argument that while positivist moral philosophy discloses that no value, purpose or interest can be justified in *a priori* or empirical terms, this disclosure does not entail anything about the *choice*, the episodic occurrence of preferring particular purposes and interests. The crucial questions in adjudication – as in morals – arise in our view not merely *about* the rules, purposes or interests, but also in connection with their *application* which requires *choices* between them. It is not contested that it is impossible to justify purposes and interests either in terms of universally accepted *a priori* norms or in terms of observable facts. The problem which judges have to face is characteristically not about purposes and interests but about the *choice* between them. Even though the rules, purposes and interests themselves cannot be justified otherwise than on personal grounds, this does not necessarily mean that it is possible to found choices *between* them only on artibary personal preferences. A statement about rules, purposes or interests does not entail a similar statement about a *choice* between such rules, purposes, or interests. The tough questions in adjudication are precisely questions about such choices.

A preference or a choice is arbitrary when no good reasons are given and when it is possible to give good reasons and when authoritative guidance is ignored. It is not arbitrary however to do what is inescapable or necessary.

The principled foundation for choices guided by rules rests in sets of commitments to apply rules in a manner compatible with the preferment of specific purposes and interests over other competing ones. These competing groups of interests give rise to recurrent inescapable alternatives, like the alternative of protecting individual free speech at the expense of a group's security, or vice versa.

The preferment of particular purposes and interests can be decided without reference to the facts of the particular cases in the context of which they arise. No amount of investigation of the facts of a case can guide the logically independent preferment of such interests. For it is in terms of such preferment that the specific consequences of the particular decision must necessarily be evaluated. The *ad hoc* balancing of interests in terms of the consequences of such balancing confuses the criterion and the object of appraisal. *Ad hoc* balancing of competing interests cannot be made by reference to the consequences of such balancing. The pretence that this is done is an instance of pseudo-pragmatism, for the consequences of a particular decision do not possess an intrinsic 'value' and cannot be evaluated except in terms of pre-postulated criteria. *Ad hoc* balancing entails the abandonment of principled and consistent decision-making.

The resolve to make principled and consistent choices·whenever possible leads to a limited number of alternatives:

i. to follow one's own commitment to prefer a specific recurring interest in its recurring clashes with other interests;

ii. to defer to the commitments of others in such circumstances whenever they can be said to exist, whether they be the commitments of exemplars, judges, drafters of legislation or commitments which can be derived from the framers of the Constitution or kindred texts such as the U.N. Charter.

The commitment of the judiciary to apply the law, to follow reason and principle rather than personal whims or preferences entails certain conclusion with respect to the permissible mode of choice between purposes and interests. The *ad hoc* balancing procedure allows judges more discretion than is necessary in the judicial system. Principled or preferred balancing faithful to that of the Framers of the Constitution can be used to replace the *ad hoc* balancing of individual judges and prevent them from substituting their own judgments for those of Congress. The *ad hoc* balancing procedure conflict, with the commitment of the judiciary to decide cases impartially, according to law and principle.

It is one thing to interpret the Constitution as a source of commitments to prefer particular purposes and interests over others, and it is another thing to interpret it as a source of specific rules. A constitutional rule requires interpretation in the context of its *application* to the *facts* of a case. It must be interpreted in the context of such facts. Not so with a statement preferring one set of interests over another. Such preferment takes place independently of the facts of a case. It is a general statement about the preferment of some interests in conflict with others which requires no application in a factual context. It need not therefore be interpreted anew from case to case. It is possible to see in the Constitution both a body of rules and a set of balances struck in favour of some interests at the expense of others. As a body of rules it requires interpretation like any other body of statutory rules. As an indication of Constitutional commitments to prefer particular interests it requires no such interpretation and the plain meaning of the words is therefore more easily capable of disclosing the nature of the commitment. It stands as a general directive to apply rules of law in a manner such that preferred interests will be respected.

A court's commitment to follow principle whenever it can find principle to guide it rather than to follow its own inclinations is precisely what is meant by the commitment to apply the rules of a system and to apply them impartially. Courts may be under a duty to seek for such principle. According to this analysis the dichotomy of rule and discretion is misleading; for on the one hand courts are never strictly bound by rules while on the other hand courts are not entirely free to choose between competing purposes and interests, since preexisting Constitutional or other commitments may be available to guide them in the application of rules. Courts which adopt the balancing expressed in the Constitution have moreover a standard for the judicial review of the activities of the executive and legislative branches of government other than their own personal preferences.

This analysis further suggests that the system of legal rules is not in any meaningful sense a 'closed' system in Kelsen's meaning and that reliance upon legal rules presupposes the related consideration of a variety of other non-legal ingredients. In considering rules as inference-guidance devices it becomes clear that it is misleading to consider them otherwise than in the context of their formulation or application. For any other approach would suggest that rules have properties independent of the contexts for which they are designed. As conceptual tools, rules are merely what they are designed to do. The 'closed' character of a system of rules is an optical or rather a conceptual illusion which occurs when they are frozen and analysed in an unspecified static heaven remote from either their promulgation or application. The hermetic quality of a system of legal rules is a myth dispelled both by a study of their making and their use.

RATIONALITY

The investigation of the concept of rule was designed to throw some fresh light on the related concept of rationality. The principal link between the two concepts can be found in the notion of consistency. For, as Wittgenstein has observed, 'The use of the word "rule" and the use of the word "same" are interwoven'. But before considering this connection any further, it might be useful to retrace in a very summary fashion some of the arguments made earlier in the book.

Reasoning guided by rules is an activity common to the fields of law and ethics. It is perhaps also at the basis of the use of words and language.

Reasoning guided by rules is not reducible to a form of deductive reasoning. By deductive reasoning we understand arguments in which the premises *necessarily* entail the conclusion. There exist systematic differences between reasoning with rules on the one hand and analytic or formal reasoning on the other. These differences arise out of a number of considerations. It is possible to formulate a major premise (rule) and a minor premise (facts) of a judicial syllogism so that it entails a necessary conclusion but this conceals the heart of the legal decision which consists in the adoption and formulation of such premises. On the other hand, formal syllogistic reasoning is purely tautological and does not entail any conclusions about the world. Moreover, in many cases competing major premises are advanced and is not possible to use syllogistic reasoning to determine which of the competing premises is the applicable one. Questions about the characterization of the facts in the minor premise of a syllogism lie beyond the province of logic and questions about the core and the penumbra of meaning of the terms used in the major premise cannot be settled by reference to other deductive syllogisms.

Nor can questions about the selection of the 'relevant' facts which make up the minor premise, from the total situation in which a choice or judgment is required, be resolved by reference to the deductive syllogism. In addition questions about factual situations not contemplated in the major premise of the syllogism such as questions involving novel factual circumstances cannot be deductively resolved by resort to premises antecedent to such circumstances. The attempt to reduce reasoning with rules to a species of deduction may lead to decisions which do violence to the requirements of justice which is one of the purposes of reasoning with rules. Such reasoning may then be self-defeating, hence irrational. This attempt also suggests that in all cases the rule applied pre-exists the decision of a case. It overlooks the reformulation of the rule in the case.

Nor is reasoning with rules reducible to a species of inductive reasoning. By inductive reasoning we understand, as Braithwaite suggests, reasoning in which an empirical generalization is inferred from instances of occurrence and reasoning which establishes a scientific hypothesis from empirical evidence for it. Inductive reasoning is reasoning supported by evidence of probability. It is reasoning about matters of fact. It is not out of place to reason inductively *about* decisions guided by rules, but it is not possible to *apply* rules inductively. 'Probability' is also relevant in the consideration of the likely consequences of a particular decision for these may colour the interpretation to be given to the applicable rule. Inductive reasoning is designed to give answers to questions about matters of fact beyond the scope of our direct, immediate knowledge and volition. It is aimed at making predictions or at drawing conclusions involving matters of fact. Reasoning with rules, on the other hand, is designed to guide decisions and judgments about matters as to which we have an option.

What sets the method of the sciences off from other methods of investigation is, to adopt Popper's suggestion, the possibility of *refuting* scientific hypotheses by experimentation. In this respect, the method of reasoning with rules is clearly extra-scientific.

Some thinkers have concluded that reasoning guided by rules is not rational and that legal opinions giving rules as reasons are in fact determined by a variety of non-rational considerations: a hunch, the personality of the judge, an emotional reaction or rhetorical arguments.

The 'validity' of formal, deductive reasoning (tautological reasoning) is predicated upon the *necessary* character of the conclusions of such reasoning. Strictly, the concept of validity has application only to individual deductive arguments or forms of deductive arguments. It is less easy to take for granted the logical foundation of inductive or scientific reasoning. It is generally admitted that it is impossible to argue with *certainty* from facts to natural laws. To show that induction is rational, without referring to the truth or the probability of its conclusions, we must discover something in induction which makes the activity worthwhile for someone who no longer expects it to yield either the certainty of deduction or the probability of the theory of chances. If we accept the rationality of induction on any one of the competing grounds offered (pragmatic – only way to make true predictions – it needs no further justification), then we necessarily reject the tentative to bring all arguments to the level of deductive logic. For such tentatives are by definition bound to fail.

Both deduction and induction possess a secure place in logical theory. The 'rationality' of the scientific method is also generally conceded. Inductive and scientific reasoning were not differentiated from formal mathematical reasoning before the work of Bacon and the British empiricists. It is not until more recently, with the work of Strawson and Toulmin that the attempt to justify induction in terms of the analytic model of reasoning has been given up. It is also well-established that the method of the natural sciences differs from the inductive method.

The abandonment of the analytic ideal in logical theory – that arguments should have the absolute certainty characteristic of tautological arguments – was brought about by the alternative between conceding Hume's position that induction can be no more than the association of ideas without logical justification or asserting that induction is rationally justified otherwise than by conforming to the analytic ideal. The abandonment of the analytic ideal means that rationality should not be understood in terms of the conformity of arguments to one ideal form of reasoning. It indicates rather that rationality is concerned with the soundness of the claims we make, with the procedures by which a scientist ought to be guided when he is engaged in research, in formulating and in verifying hypotheses, and that reasoning about reasoning is rational without being either deductive or inductive; that logic is concerned with the criteria for the rationality of arguments in a given field, as well as with the reasons for employing such criteria, and with the necessary relations between the concepts used in a particular discipline and the necessary implications of procedures adopted.

Since reasoning guided by rules is not reducible either to deductive reasoning, nor to inductive and scientific reasoning, it is either not rational or rationality consists also of at least another form of reasoning.

We have here attempted to elaborate some of the elements of another kind of logic distinct from deduction, induction and the scientific method – a working logic. It is a logic, as Toulmin suggested, concerned with substantive or non-analytic arguments, it is field-dependent and requires a careful definition of the field of arguments to which it applies. In connection with legal and ethical reasoning, for example, there are a number of possible delimitations of such applicable field: the field of decision-making, the field of legal argument, the field of moral choice or the field of reasoning with rules. We selected the field of reasoning with rules, since it displays necessary connections and inevitable relationships between rules, facts, purposes and unavoidable options for choosing between them.

The formulation of the logic of reasoning with rules expresses the recurring necessary connections between rules and other elements of separate logical texture which are necessarily involved in the *application* of such rules. Yet it is distinct from Deontic Logic which is the logic founded upon the premise that rules can logically contradict one another independently of their application. Such a premise necessarily entails the formulation of another premise about the unity and coherence of a will from which rules originate. We do not share these premises.

The elements of separate logical texture which are necessarily involved in the application of rules can perhaps be outlined graphically more effectively than they can be listed. They involve, broadly speaking, six principal categories: (i) fact statements, (ii) law statements – guidance devices, (iii) processes of reasoning, (iv) statement of the decision reached, (v) statement of the foreseeable consequences of the decision reached, (vi) statement of the foreseeable future application of the law statements. These separate elements belong to clearly heterogeneous domains, to clearly separate realms of discourse, yet they are all implicated in the process of following or applying a rule. More specifically these categories can be broken down into a number of distinct ingredients:

    i. the facts on record (F),

    ii. the competing preexisting rules or precedents (L) and (L').

    iii. the process of (a) selecting the material facts and (b) reasoning from the material facts to the required or desired conclusion (I),

    iv. the statement about the process or reasoning just referred to (SI),

    v. the formulation of the rule governing the case being decided on the basis of preexisting rules or precedents (SL),

    vi. the decision, order or other final disposition of the case (D),

    vii. the foreseeable consequences of the decision (CD),

    viii. the foreseeable range of application of the rule formulated in the case (supra v.) in other cases and their foreseeable consequences (CSL),

    ix. the competing canons for the construction of rules and the competing techniques for using precedents (IN) and (IN')

    x. the purposes and interests contemplated by the preexisting rules (L), the newly formulated rules (SL) and the canons of construction (IN). These are here referred to as (P),

    xi. competing such purposes and interests (P'),

    xii. the preexisting commitments to weigh the competing purposes and interests in favour of specific purposes (P) whenever a conflict between recurring purposes and interests arises. This commitment

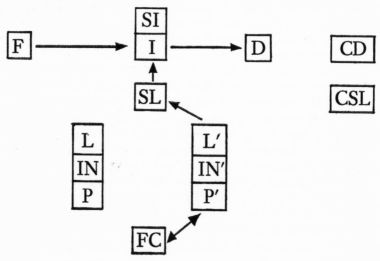

in turn depends upon another distinct commitment to follow pre-existing authority whenever such guidance is available. It is a peculiarly judicial commitment (FC).

The relationship between these disparate and yet related elements is a very close one. The concept of rule presupposes contexts of application. It is a purposive concept, designed to promote ends and policies. As such, its proper use requires that great weight be attached to the consequences of application. For applications of rules which are destructive of their policy ends are essentially irrational. Moreover, the use of rules is accompanied by the phenomenon that competing and rival interpretations are frequently unavoidable. This phenomenon arises either because of the irreducible problem of the 'core' and 'penumbra' of meaning characteristic of language generally, or because particular applications may be marginal with respect to the purposes of relevant rules. The difficulties are unavoidably compounded when more than one rule is applicable in any given situation. The difficulties which surround the application of rules can be formally resolved by reference to the technical rules for the construction of statutes or for the use of precedents. But such decisions substantially also involve choices between unavoidably proliferating purposes and policies. They also impose a procedural option involving the mode of choice between rival purposes and policies; between decisions guided by principle and unprincipled choice.

The relationship between these disparate elements is dominated by the demands of *necessary* presuppositions, implications and consequences. These come as close as can be expected to the necessary features of formal logic in a field which involves substantive arguments, i.e. arguments that are not tautological.

The soundness of arguments in rule-guided fields can be ascertained by the extent to which they do not disregard these necessary features. This suggests that rational arguments in this field are those that lead to decisions and choices made in reliance on inference-guidance devices with proper regard for the necessary presuppositions, implications, consequences and other features unavoidable in the use of these devices.

These features of rule-guided reasoning provide the basis for the articulation of a standard model of rationality other than the logico-mathematical model on the one hand and the scientific model on the other. They meet the requirements generally associated with rationality. Thus one of the demands of rationality most often emphasized is the requirement of consistency. The concept of rule is designed to make consistent choices and decisions possible. It imports the variety of factors which provide a context for the use of the concept of consistency: facts, consequences, purposes, policies and principled guidance. The concepts of rule and consistency are so closely intertwined that to say of a decision that it is principled but inconsistent would involve a contradictory usage of these concepts. Another important demand of rationality is that means be appropriate for the ends they are designed to promote, this is the prudential quality required of function-serving decision-making. Rationality demands that consequences of contemplated applications be appraised by reference to operative purposes and policies; it thus establishes an equilibrium in the means – end continuum by underscoring not only the consequences of desired ends but also of the means for attaining them. This particular demand of rationality is backed by the check of refutability, since conjectures about consequences are frequently refutable by observation. The demand that decisions and choices be as unarbitrary as possible can be equated with the demand that they be consistent and principled whenever possible. Rationality can thus in a large measure be equated with reasoning relying upon inference-guidance devices which respects their necessary features and the unavoidable boundaries confronted in their use. Rational arguments involve a *sequence* of mental operations reflecting the guidance features of rules, principles, purposes and policies. Guided reasoning is thus bounded by necessary relations, implications and consequences and also by unavoidable options. The notion of conceptual boundary reflects the hard compulsions of necessity encountered in tautological arguments. However, guided or rational reasoning is itself not necessary. Rational argument involves opting for rationality which is but one of competing mental procedures. While that particular opting is not unavoidable, the option itself is wholly necessary.

Rational rule-guided choices and decisions are neither founded upon *a priori* nor upon empirical grounds. This does not mean that they rest in the last analysis upon arbitrary personal preferences or that they are exlusively conventional. Rule guided choices and decisions ideally rest in the last resort upon *deference* to preferred balancings between rival purposes and policies although in numerous instances there may be none to defer to. This leaves open questions about the foundations of 'preferred balancings' themselves which do not lie within the province of this book. Similarly, questions about justifications for the adoption or formulation of rules and other inference-guidance devices also transcend the problems involving their use and application with which we have been concerned here. We propose to explore in another work both the necessary boundaries of clashes between recurring conflicting ends as well the unavoidable procedural options between consistency, deference to exemplars, conversion to inconsistent balancings and un-principled choices which are involved in the adoption of guidance devices.

Rule-guided reasoning – or the logic of choice – is an alternative to the analytic and scientific methods on the one hand and to meta-physical thought on the other. It is of direct relevance to all the disciplines concerned with reasoned choice and decision-making. It is a method proper to the fields of reasoned, guided deliberation. The logic of choice thus provides the conceptual framework for the systematic criticism of the application of rules and principles in systems purporting to place reliance upon them.

The fields relying upon rules for guidance are numerous. This analysis of the concepts of rule and rationality was made primarily on the basis of the function of rules in law and in ethics. Yet rules occupy an equally central position in logical and in mathematical theory, in grammar and in the very institution of language. The connection between the role of rules in these separate fields has not been explored, but it does suggest a methodological unity. It is manifest that the concepts of rule and rationality are intimately related. This should be encouraging to scholars in rule-guided fields who have been resisting demands to recast all knowledge into either foimal knowledge modelled upon mathematics or scientific knowl-edge modelled upon the natural sciences; for reasoning may be rational without being either analytic or scientific.

NOTES

The following notes are designed to give the sources of quotations and references to cited materials. In addition, these notes refer to some contemporary writings which have a bearing on the views discussed in the text.

CHAPTER II

[1] Cardozo, *The Nature of the Judicial Process*, 10, 11 (1921).

[2] Konstam, J., in 'Acceptance of Rent after Notice to Quit', 60 *L.Q. Rev.*, 232 (1944).

[3] Lawson, *The Rational Strength of English Law*, 79-80 (1951), see also the excellent article of Pound in *Science of Legal Method*, 202, 211 (1917) who notes that both Bentham and Austin believed in the possibility of a perfect code; see thus Bentham, *Constitutional Code* (1830) and volume X of the Bowring edition (1843), and see 2 Austin, *Jurisprudence*, 695 (4th ed.). For a good statement of the intentions of the code-makers of Frederic the Great, see Schuster, 'The German Civil Code', 12 *L.Q. Rev.*, 17 (1896).

[4] Mill, *A System of Logic*, 616 f. (Longman ed. 1930).

[5] For a full and critical account of this period of legal history see Stone, *Legal System and Lawyers' Reasonings*, ch. 6 (1964).

[6] Wasserstrom, *The Judicial Decision*, 15 (1961) for a concise summary of the role of deduction in legal theory; see also Carruccio, *Mathematics and Logic in History and in Contemporary Thought* (1964).

[7] Toulmin, *The Uses of Argument*, 122 (1958) for a discussion of the role played by deductive arguments in epistemological theory.

[8] Wittgenstein, *Tractatus Logico-Philosophicus*, 155, 163 (1922), hereinafter *Tractatus*.

[9] Hart, 'Positivism and the Separation of Law and Morals', 71 *Harv. L. Rev.*, 593, 610 (1958).

[10] Allen, *Law in the Making*, 154 (5th ed. 1951).

[11] *id.*, 155.

[12] Paton, *Jurisprudence*, 152 (2nd ed. 1951).

[13] Kneale, *Probability and Induction*, 104–5 (1949).

[14] Braithwaite, *Scientific Explanation*, 257 (1953).

[15] Strawson, *Introduction to Logical Theory*, 237 (1952).

[16] *Tractatus*, 181.

[17] Toulmin, *The Philosophy of Science* (1953) for a discussion of the functions and uses of scientific laws.

[18] Paton, *supra.*, n. 12 at 152, 153.

[19] Holmes, *Collected Legal Papers*, 173 (1920).

[20] Cook, 'Scientific Method and the Law', 13 *A.B.A.J.*, 303, 308 (1927).

[21] *Tractatus*, §§6.53, 6.54, 7.

[22] Keyser, 'On the Study of Legal Science', 38 *Yale L.J.*, 413, 415 (1929).

[23] Popper, *Conjectures and Refutations*, 33 (1963) and also his *The Logic of Scientific Discovery*, 40 (1959).

[24] On Austin's theory see Stone, n. 5 *supra*., at 312; on C. S. Peirce's theory of abduction see his V *Collected Papers*, 105 f. (1921–58). On Dewey's theory see 'Logical Method and Law', *infra*., n. 25. For Perelman's work see *Traité de L'Argumentation* (1958) and *The Idea of Justice and the Problem of Argument* (1963). For Bobbio's many valued normative analysis see his *Teoria Della Norma Giuridica* (1958). von Wright's position is conveniently stated in *Norm and Action* (1963) and in *The Varieties of Goodness* (1963) and Wasserstrom's theory in *The Judicial Decision* (1961).

[25] See Dewey's essay 'Logical Method and Law', 10 *Cornell L.Q.*, 17 (1924) and *Essays in Experimental Logic* (1916).

[26] Wasserstrom, *supra*., n. 6 at 23.

[27] For convenient excerpts of relevant writings see Cohen and Cohen, *Readings in Jurisprudence and Legal Philosophy* (1951).

[28] Frank, *Law and the Modern Mind*, 111 (1930).

[29] For an important discussion of the realist movement see Hart, *The Concept of Law*, ch. VII (1961).

[30] Llewellyn, *The Common Law Tradition*, 4 f. (1960).

[31] See Oppenheimer, 'The Age of Science 1900–1950', 183 *Scientific American*, 20, 22 (1950) cited in Richards *infra*., note 32.

[32] Richards, *Speculative Instruments*, 114 (1955).

[33] Strawson, *supra*., n. 15 at 249.

[34] Descartes, *Oeuvres*, 571 (Pleiades ed. 1953).

[35] 2 Hume, *Treatise of Human Nature*, 167–8 (Lindsay ed. 1911) (in bk. iii, sec. 1).

[36] Toulmin, *supra*., n. 7 at 250.

[37] See Toulmin, *id*., ch. IV and Strawson, *supra*., n. 15 at 256.

[38] See Waismann, 'Verifiability' in Flew, *Logic and Language*, 1st Series, 117 (1951).

[39] Ryle, *Dilemmas*, 42 (1954).

[40] Urmson, in Flew, *Essays in Conceptual Analysis*, 132–3 (1956).

[41] Wittgenstein, *Philosophical Investigations*, #23 (1953).

[42] cf. Popper, *The Logic of Scientific Discovery*, 51 n. (1959).

[43] Wisdom, 'Gods', in Flew, *Logic and Language*, 1st Series, 187, 195 (1951).

[44] Toulmin, *supra*., n. 7 at 188.

[45] 4 Bacon, *Works*, 451 (Spedding ed. 1901).

[46] Ayer, *Language, Truth and Logic*, 100 (1936).

CHAPTER III

[1] Austin, *Philosophical Papers*, 220 (1961).

[2] Ryle, *The Concept of Mind*, 121–2 (1949).

[3] Wittgenstein, *Philosophical Investigations*, #85, #228 (1953); Hart, *The Concept of Law*, 55–6, 86–8, 242, 244 (1961); and Winch, *The Idea of a Social Science*, 25–39 (1958).

[4] Austin, *The Province of Jurisprudence Determined*, 13 (1954 ed.).

[5] von Wright, *Norm and Action*, 102 (1963).

[6] Feigl, 'Logical Empiricism' in Feigl and Sellars, *Readings in Philosophical Analysis*, 10-11 (1949).

[7] Hägerström, *Inquiries into the Nature of Law and Morals*, 4, 16 (1953).

[8] Hart, H. L. A., *Definition and Theory in Jurisprudence*, 70 *L.Q. Rev.*, 37 (1954).

[9] Wittgenstein, *Philosophical Investigations*, #66, #67 (1958); see also Khatchadorian, 'Common Names' and 'Family Resemblances', in Pitcher ed., *Wittgenstein, The Philosophical Investigations*, 205 (1966).

[10] Hart, *The Concept of Law*, 8-9, 14-15 (1961). Hart's position is best understood with Winch, *The Idea of a Social Science* (1958) and Waismann, *The Principles of Linguistic Philosophy*, ch. VII (1965); see also particularly Black, *Models and Metaphors* (1962), von Wright, *The Varieties of Goodness*, ch. VIII (1963), and the important essay of Rawls, 'Two Concepts of Rules', 64 *Phil. Rev.*, 3 (1955). See the discussion of the relationship between rationality and rules in Bennett, *Rationality*, 15 f., 56 f. (1964) and the analysis of Wittgenstein's philosophy by Pitcher, *The Philosophy of Wittgenstein* (1964) and by Pole, *The Later Philosophy of Wittgenstein*, 29 f., 55 f. (1958).

[11] Black, *Models and Metaphors*, 104-6 (1962); but see the discussion in Rescher, *The Logic of Commands* (1966).

[12] See von Wright, *Norm and Action*, ch. VI (1963), and Austin, *Philosophical Papers*, 230 (1961) as well as Black, *Models and Metaphors*, 125-8 (1962) and Rescher, *The Logic of Commands*, 8 f. (1966).

[13] Wittgenstein, *Philosophical Investigations*, #89 ff. (1953) and see generally Pole, *The Later Philosophy of Wittgenstein*, 29 ff. (1958).

[14] Wittgenstein, *Philosophical Investigations*, #108 (1953).

[15] Fuller, *The Morality of Law*, 33 ff. (1964).

[16] See Singer, 'Moral Rules and Principles', in Melden ed., *Essays in Moral Philosophy*, 160 (1958).

[17] *R. v. Macallister*, (1808), C.C.C. Sess. Pap. LXXXVI, 18, cited in Kenny, *Outlines of Criminal Law*, 208 (15 ed. 1946).

[18] Cited in I. Blackstone, *Commentaries on the Laws of England*, *61.

[19] Northrop, *The Complexity of Legal and Ethical Experience*, 189 (1959).

[20] 'Four Quartets', Eliot, *Collected Poems*, 1909-62, 180 (1963).

[21] Flew, *Logic and Language*, 1st Series, 117 (1951), Waismann, 'Verifiability'. In this context note H. L. A. Hart's discussion of the Open Texture of Law in *The Concept of Law*, 121 ff.

[22] In Flew, *ibid*.

CHAPTER IV

[1] Hampshire, 'Fallacies in Moral Philosophy', 58 *Mind*, 476 (1949). See also Austin, *Philosophical Papers*, ch. 5 (1961); Sup. Vol. XXIV, *Proc'd'gs Aristotelian Soc'y* (1950), and von Wright, *Norm and Action*, 25 f. (1963) as well as the excellent collection of essays in Pitcher (ed.), *Truth* (1964).

[2] Camus, *Discours de Suède*, 43, 46 (1958); my own translation.

[3] Richards, *Speculative Instruments*, 139 (1955).

[4] Aristotle, *Ethics*, bk. vi, ch. ix at 184 (Penguin ed. 1953).

[5] Frank, *Courts on Trial*, 326 (1949).

[6] Waismann, 'Verifiability', in Flew, *Logic and Language*, 1st Series, 122–3 (1951); see also Hampshire, *Thought and Action*, 22 (1959).

[7] Wittgenstein, *Philosophical Investigations*, #68 (1953).

[8] Black, *Models and Metaphors*, 124 (1962).

[9] Waismann, 'Verifiability', in Flew, *Logic and Language*, 1st Series, 129 (1951).

[10] Hart, H. L. A., 'The Ascription of Responsibility and Rights', in Flew, *Logic and Language*, 1st Series, 145 (1951).

[11] *Smith v. Hiatt*, 329 Mass. 488 (1952) and the background to this case considered in Hart and Sacks, *The Legal Process*, 1226 (1958).

[12] Wittgenstein, *Philosophical Investigations*, #129 (1953).

[13] Hart H., and McNaughton, 'Evidence and Inference in the Law', in 87 *Daedalus*, 53 (1958).

[14] *Gideon v. Wainwright*, 372 U.S., 335 (1963), Lewis, *Gideon's Trumpet* (1964).

[15] Myrdal, *Value in Social Theory*, xxvii (1958) from the introduction by Paul Streeten.

[16] *id.*, 132.

[17] Polanyi, *Personal Knowledge*, ch. I (1958).

CHAPTER V

[1] Ryle, *The Concept of Mind*, 138 (1949).

[2] *id.*, 140.

[3] Wittgenstein, *Philosophical Investigations*, #228 (1953).

[4] *id.*, #172.

[5] *id.*, #170.

[6] *id.*, #155, and see Wittgenstein, *The Blue and Brown Books*, 3 (1958). See also Ryle, *The Concept of Mind*, 135 f. (1949) and see for a discussion of Wittgenstein's and Ryle's position, Geach, *Mental Acts* (1957). See further the useful discussion in Pitcher, *The Philosophy of Wittgenstein*, ch. 11 (1964).

[7] Wittgenstein, *Philosophical Investigations*, #169 (1953).

[8] Hart, *The Concept of Law*, 55–6 (1961).

[9] Wittgenstein, *Philosophical Investigations*, #156 f. (1953).

[10] Waismann, 'Verifiability', in Flew, *Logic and Language*, 1st Series, 128 (1951).

[11] Cardozo, *The Nature of the Judicial Process*, 164 (1921).

[12] See *infra.*, p. 83.

[13] Llewellyn, *The Common Law Tradition*, 131 (1960).

[14] 4 *Q.B.D.* (1881); see also *Taylor v. Goodwin* (1879), 4 *Q.B.D.*, 228.

[15] Black, *Models and Metaphors*, 125 f. (1962) and Wittgenstein, *Philosophical Investigations*, #201 (1955).

[16] Llewellyn, *The Common Law Tradition*, 110 (1960).

[17] 283 U.S., 25 (1939); see also Hart and Sacks, *The Legal Process*, 1231 (1958); for interestingly similar English cases see Paton, *Jurisprudence*, 167 (2nd ed., 1951).

[18] Wittgenstein, *The Philosophical Investigations*, #201 (1953).

[19] Dewey, *Essays in Experimental Logic*, ch. XIV (1916).

[20] See Lewis, *Gideon's Trumpet* (1964).

M

[21] 316 U.S., 455 (1941).
[22] Oldenquist, 'Rules and Consequences', 75 *Mind*, 180 (1966); see also 65 *Proc'd'gs Aristotelian Soc'y*, 147 f. (1964-5) and von Wright, *Norm and Action*, 39 f. (1963).
[23] Wechsler, 'Toward Neutral Principles of Constitutional Law', 73 *Harv. L. Rev.*, 1 (1959). See also in Hook (ed.), *Law and Philosophy*, 301 (1964) for Henkin's discussion of Wechsler argument.
[24] In Hook (ed.), *Law and Philosophy*, 297 (1964).
[25] *id.*, 263 at 274.
[26] *id.*, 301 at 306.

CHAPTER VI

[1] The groundwork for this distinction has been laid in ch. V *supra*.
[2] Llewellyn, *The Common Law Tradition*, 77 f. (1960).
[3] See the discussions by Montrose, Simpson and Goodhart in 20 *Mod. L. Rev.*, 587 (1957); 21 *Mod. L. Rev.*, 155 (1958); and 22 *Mod. L. Rev.*, 117 (1959); and also J. Stone's contribution in 22 *Mod. L. Rev.*, 597 (1959).
[4] Stone, *The Province and Function of Law*, 187 (1950 ed.).
[5] Goodhart, 'Determining the Ratio Decidendi of a Case', 40 *Yale L.J.*, 161 (1930).
[6] Stone, 'The Ratio of the Ratio Decidendi', 22 *Mod. L. Rev.*, 597, 602 (1959).
[7] Goodhart, 'The Ratio Decidendi of a Case', 22 *Mod. L. Rev.*, 117, 122, 119 (1955).
[8] Stone, 'The Ratio of the Ratio Decidendi', 22 *Mod. L. Rev.*, 597, 603 (1959).
[9] [1955] N.I. 112 cited by Montrose in 20 *Mod. L. Rev.*, 124, 125 (1957).
[10] Goodhart, 'The Ratio Decidendi of a Case', 22 *Mod. L. Rev.*, 117 (1959).
[11] Simpson, 'The Ratio Decidendi of a Case', 22 *Mod. L. Rev.*, 453, 454 (1959).
[12] [1932] A.C. at 580.
[13] 1 Blackstone, *Commentaries on the Laws of England*, *71 (6th ed., 1765).
[14] Goodhart at 22 *Mod. L. Rev.*, 119 (1959).
[15] Montrose at 20 *Mod. L. Rev.*, 124 (1957).
[16] Montrose in 20 *Mod. L. Rev.*, 587, 588 (1957).
[17] Stone, *The Province and Function of Law*, 187 (1950 ed.).
[18] Wasserstrom, *The Judicial Decision*, 53 f. (1961).
[19] Goodhart at 22 *Mod. L. Rev.*, 119 (1959).
[20] *ibid.*
[21] Stone, *Legal System and Lawyers' Reasonings*, 272 (1964).
[22] *id.*, at 274.
[23] Stone, 'The Ratio of the Ratio Decidendi, 22 *Mod. L. Rev.*, 597, 604 (1959).
[24] Levi in Hook (ed.), *Law and Philosophy*, 263 (1964).
[25] Stone, *Legal System and Lawyers' Reasonings*, 278 f. (1964).
[26] Wechsler in Hook (ed.), *Law and Philosophy*, 298 (1964).
[27] On this subject, see ch. VIII below.
[28] Salmond, *Jurisprudence*, 175 (3rd ed. 1910).

[29] Kelsen, *General Theory of Law and State*, 134-5 (1945).

[30] Wright, *Legal Essays and Addresses*, xvi (1939), and see Stone, *Legal System and Lawyers' Reasonings*, 129 f. (1964).

[31] Ford, *Robe and Sword* (1953) for an excellent discussion of French courts in the eighteenth century.

[32] *The Federalist*, #78.

[33] Allen, *Law in the Making*, 267 (5th ed. 1951).

[34] Friedmann, 'Legal Philosophy and Judicial Law Making', 61 *Col. L. Rev.*, 821 (1961).

CHAPTER VII

[1] Allen, *Law in the Making*, 500 (5th ed. 1951).

[2] Curtis, 'A Better Theory of Legal Interpretation', 3 *Vand. L. Rev.*, 407 (1950); see also the important treatise Sutherland, *Statutes and Statutory Construction* (3rd ed. 1943), and the excellent analysis in Hart and Sacks, *The Legal Process*, ch. VII (1958).

[3] Llewellyn, *The Common Law Tradition*, 24-6, 226 (1960) for a discussion of the unhappy effects of the 'single right answer' doctrine of interpretation.

[4] See the still excellent essay by Kohler, 'Judicial Interpretation of Enacted Law', in *Science of Legal Method*, 187 (1917).

[5] *Thockmerton v. Tracy*, 1 Plow., 145, 162, 75 *Eng. Rep.*, 222, 251 (K.B. 1554) cited in Curtis at 408.

[6] Frankfurter, 'Some Reflections on the Reading of Statutes', 47 *Col. L. Rev.*, 527 (1947) reprinted in his *Of Law and Men*, 44 (1956). See also Holmes' discussion of the place of intention in the construction of legal instruments in Holmes, *Collected Legal Papers*, 203-4 (1920); see further MacCallum, 'Legislative Intent', 75 *Yale L.J.*, 754 (1966).

[7] In *Doe ex dem. Hick v. Dring*, 2 M.&S., 448, 455, 105 *Eng. Rep.*, 447, 450 (K.B. 1814) cited in Curtis at 409.

[8] Curtis, 'A Better Theory of Legal Interpretation', 3 *Vand. L. Rev.*, 407, 409 (1950).

[9] 288 U.S., 280, 285 (1933).

[10] 139 F. 2d., 809, 823 (2nd Cir. 1943).

[11] 47 F. Supp., 251 (S.D.W.Va. 1942).

[12] Reprinted in *Collected Legal Papers*, 203, 204 (1920).

[13] Curtis at 3 *Vand. L. Rev.*, 419 (1950).

[14] From Kelsen, *Reine Rechtslehre* cited in Ebenstein, *The Pure Theory of Law*, 194 (1945).

[15] Frankfurter, 'Some Reflections on the Reading of Statutes', 47 *Col. L. Rev.*, 527, 534 (1947).

[16] Hampshire, 'Logic and Appreciation', in Elton, *Aesthetics and Language*, 162 (1954); see also Cioffi, 'Intention and Interpretation in Criticism', 64 *Proc'd'gs Aristotelian Soc'y*, 85 (1964).

[17] Hampshire, *id.*, at 168.

[18] Kelsen, *The Law of the United Nations* (1950).

[19] Kemeny, 'A Philosopher Looks at Political Science', 4 *J. Conflict Resolution*, 292 (1960).

[20] 14 *Q.B.D.*, 273 (1884).
[21] Curtis, 'A Better Theory of Legal Interpretation', 3 *Vand. L. Rev.*, 407, 424 (1950).
[22] Curtis, *id.*, at 422.
[23] Frankfurter, 'Some Reflections on the Reading of Statutes', 47 *Col. L. Rev.*, 527, 543 (1947).
[24] Wurzel, 'Methods of Juridical Thinking', *Science of Legal Method*, 286, 307 (1917).
[25] Llewellyn, *The Common Law Tradition*, 77 f. (1960).
[26] Wurzel, in *Science of Legal Method*, 311 (1917).
[27] Wurzel, *ibid.*
[28] Llewellyn, 'Remarks on the Theory of Appellate Decision and on the Rules or Canons About How Statutes Are to be Construed', 3 *Vand. L. Rev.*, 395, 401 (1950).
[29] Frankfurter, 'Some Reflections on the Reading of Statutes', 47 *Col. L. Rev.*, 527, 544 (1947).
[30] Wittgenstein, *Philosophical Investigations*, #84 (1953).

CHAPTER VIII

[1] Fuller, *The Morality of Law*, 146 (1964). See Hart's interesting review of the book in 78 *Harv. L. Rev.*, 1281 (1965).
[2] Wasserstrom, *The Judicial Decision*, 10–11 (1961).
[3] Dworkin, 'Does Law Have a Function?', 74 *Yale L.J.*, 640, 646 (1965).
[4] Hart, *The Concept of Law*, 189 f. (1961).
[5] Hart, 'Positivism and the Separation of Law and Morals', 71 *Harv. L. Rev.*, 593, 608 (1958).
[6] Fuller, 'Positivism and Fidelity to Law – A Reply to Professor Hart', 71 *Harv. L. Rev.*, 630, 663 (1958).
[7] *id.*, at 666.
[8] Hughes, 'The Existence of a Legal System', 35 *N.Y.U. L. Rev.*, 1001, 1024 (1960).
[9] *id.*, at 1025.
[10] Fuller, 'Human Purpose and Natural Law', 3 *Natural L. Forum*, 68 (1958); see also Nagel, 'On the Fusion of Fact and Value: A Reply to Professor Fuller', *id.*, at 77, and Fuller, 'A Rejoinder to Professor Nagel', *id.*, at 83.
[11] The example is borrowed from the Fuller-Hart exchange in 71 *Harv. L. Rev.*, at 663.
[12] Hart, *The Concept of Law*, 125 (1961).
[13] Frankfurter, 'Some Reflections on the Reading of Statutes', 47 *Col. L. Rev.*, 527, 539 (1947).
[14] Fuller, in 3 *Natural L. Forum* at 71. The literature on purpose and policy is growing rapidly. See notably Taylor, *The Explanation of Behaviour* (1964), and the review by Malcolm in 76 *Phil. Rev.*, 97 (1967); Dworkin, 'Philosophy, Morality and Law', 113 *U. Pa. L. Rev.*, 668 (1965); Austin, 'Three Ways of Spilling Ink', 75 *Phil. Rev.*, 427 (1966); VII *Nomos, Rational Decision* (1964); Gibson, *The Logic of Social Inquiry* (1960) and Barry, *Political Argument* (1965); note Kenny, 'Intention and Purpose', 53 *J. Phil.*, 642 (1966).

The uses of the concepts purpose, policy and interest often overlap. For discussions of the concept of interest see ch. X, n. 17 *infra*.

15 Wittgenstein, *Philosophical Investigations*, 33e (1953).
16 Dewey, *Human Nature and Conduct*, 232 (1930 ed.); see also Kolnai, 'Deliberation is of Ends', 62 *Proc'd'gs Aristotelian Soc'y*, 195 (1962).
17 Fuller, in 3 *Natural L. Forum* at 96 f.
18 Curtis, 'A Better Theory of Legal Interpretation', 3 *Vand. L. Rev.*, 407, 422, 423 (1950).
19 Wittgenstein, *Philosophical Investigations*, #199 (1953).
20 Austin, *The Province of Jurisprudence Determined*, 350 (1954 ed.).
21 Hand, *The Bill of Rights*, 4 (1958).
22 Austin, *The Province of Jurisprudence Determined*, 21 (1954 ed.).
23 For a recent characteristic statement, McDougal, 'Jurisprudence in a Free Society', 1 *Geo. L. Rev.*, 1, 15 (1966).
24 Friedmann, 'Legal Philosophy and Judicial Law Making', 61 *Col. L. Rev.*, 821, 842 (1961).
25 Rostow, *The Sovereign Prerogative*, 28 (1962).
26 Dworkin, 'Judicial Discretion', 60 *J. Phil.*, 624 (1963).
27 The theories of Lasswell and McDougal have had a profound impact on American thinking. See notably McDougal, 'Law as a Process of Decision: A Policy-Oriented Approach to Legal Study', 1 *Natural L. Forum*, 53 (1956); McDougal and Feliciano, *Law and Minimum World Public Order* (1961); McDougal, 'International Law Power and Policy: A Contemporary Conception', 82 *Hague Receuil*, 137 (1952), see also for discussions of these theories a book review by Falk, 8 *Natural L. Forum*, 171 (1963), Anderson, 'A Critique of Professor Myres R. McDougal's 'Doctrine of Interpretation by Major Purposes', 57 *A.J. Int'l L.*, 378 (1963), and Falk, 'The Adequacy of Contemporary Theories of International Law – Gaps in Legal Thinking', 50 *Va. L. Rev.*, 231 (1964).

CHAPTER IX

1 Hart, *The Concept of Law*, 114 f. (1961).
2 Hart, *The Concept of Law*, 60–4 (1961); see also the comments of Fuller, *The Morality of Law*, 141 f. (1964).
3 Kelsen, *General Theory of Law and State*, 39 (1945).
4 Wittgenstein, *Philosophical Investigations*, #121 (1953).
5 United Nations General Assembly Resolution 95 (I).
6 Hart, *The Concept of Law*, 114 f. (1961).
7 *id.*, 108.
8 *id.*, 77–96.
9 *id.*, 205.
10 Hart, 'Book Review: The Morality of Law', 78 *Harv. L. Rev.*, 1281, 1294 (1965).
11 Fuller, *The Morality of Law*, 148 f. (1964).
12 Fuller, 'Positivism and Fidelity to Law – A Reply to Professor Hart, 71 *Harv. L. Rev.*, 630, 666 (1958), and Hart, 'Positivism and the Separation of Law and Morals', 71 *Harv. L. Rev.*, 593, 608 (1958).

CHAPTER X

[1] The Supreme Court has been criticised for being unprincipled in its opinions notably by Wechsler, 'Towards Neutral Principles of Constitutional Law', 73 *Harv. L. Rev.*, 1 (1959), and by Bickel, *The Least Dangerous Branch* (1962) and *Politics and the Warren Court* (1965). See also Reich, 'Mr. Justice Black and the Living Constitution', 76 *Harv. L. Rev.*, 673 (1963).

[2] Rostow, *The Sovereign Prerogative*, 13–17, 26 f. (1962).

[3] Ch. VIII *supra*.

[4] 2 Jaspers, *Philosophie*, ch. 7 (1932). See also Wild, *The Challenge of Existentialism*, 80 f., 139 f., 153, 214–15 (1955).

[5] Reich, 'Mr. Justice Black and the Living Constitution', 76 *Harv. L. Rev.*, 673, 736 (1963).

[6] Freund, *The Supreme Court of the United States*, ch. VII (1949).

[7] 366 U.S., 36, 50–51 (1961).

[8] Brennan, 'The Supreme Court and the Meiklejohn Interpretation of the First Amendment', 79 *Harv. L. Rev.*, 1, 11 (1965).

[9] *ibid.*, see also McKay, 'The Preference For Freedom', 34 *N.Y.U.L. Rev.*, 1182 (1959).

[10] 383 U.S., 436, 480 (1966).

[11] 183 F.2d., 201, 212 aff'd; 341 U.S., 494, 510 (1951).

[12] Freund, *On Understanding the Supreme Court*, 27, 28 (1949).

[13] Reich, 'Mr. Justice Black and the Living Constitution', 76 *Harv. L. Rev.*, 673, 737 (1963).

[14] 383 U.S., 436, 477 (1966); see also Emerson, 'Toward a General Theory of the First Amendment', 72 *Yale L. J.*, 877, 913 (1963).

[15] Fuller, *The Morality of Law*, 33-8 (1964).

[16] Meiklejohn, 'The First Amendment is an Absolute', 1961 *Supreme Court Review*, 245 (Kurland ed.).

[17] See Reich, in 76 *Yale L. J.* at 719. The concepts of purpose, policy and interest are closely interwoven. See n. 14, ch. VIII *supra*. On the concept of interest see Stone, *Social Dimensions of Law and Justice*, ch. 4, 5, 6 (1966), and Fried, 'Two Concepts of Interests: Some Reflections on the Supreme Court's Balancing Test', 76 *Harv. L. Rev.*, 755 (1963); the symposium in Sup. Vol. 38 *Proc'd'gs Aristotelian Soc'y*, 1 (1964); Schubert, *The Public Interest: A Critique of the Theory of a Political Concept* (1960); Barry, *Political Argument* (1965); Benn, 'Interests in Politics', 60 *Proc'd'gs Aristotelian Soc'y*, 123 (1960). Plamenatz, 'Interests', 2 *Political Studies*, 1 (1954); Hare, *Freedom and Reason*, 101–5, 145–80 (1963); and finally the excellent collection of essays in V *Nomos, The Public Interest* (1962), as well as Leys and Perry, *Philosophy and the Public Interest*, (1959).

[18] See Stone, *The Province and Function of Law*, 493 (1950) citing Pound, 'A Survey of Social Interests', 57 *Harv. L. Rev.*, 1 (1943).

[19] 360 U.S., 109, 144 (1959) and see Reich, 76 *Harv. L. Rev.*, 719.

[20] Stone, *Social Dimensions of Law and Justice*, ch. 4, 5, 6 (1966).

[21] 366 U.S., 36, 75 (1961).

[22] cited in W. W. Bartley, *The Retreat to Commitment*, viii (1962) from 1960 *Philosophy*, April issue, 'Notes on Philosophy', January 1960.

[23] Fried, 'Two Concepts of Interests: Some Reflections on the Supreme Court's Balancing Test', 76 *Harv. L. Rev.*, 755 (1963).

[24] Wechsler, 'Toward Neutral Principles of Constitutional Law', 73 *Harv. L. Rev.*, 1, 19 (1959).

[25] *id.*, at 40; see also Dworkin, 'Judicial Discretion', 60 *J. Phil.*, 624 (1963).

[26] Golding, 'Principled Decision-Making and the Supreme Court', 63 *Col. L. Rev.*, 35, 44 (1963).

[27] Kelsen, *What is Justice?*, 141 (1957).

[28] Aiken, *Reason and Conduct*, 104 (1962).

[29] *id.*, 104–5.

[30] Sartre, *L'Existentialisme est un Humanisme*, 37 (1960 ed.).

[31] Wittgenstein, *Philosophical Investigations*, #217 (1953).

[32] Golding, 'Principled Decision-Making and the Supreme Court', 63 *Col. L. Rev.*, 35, 48–9 (1963).

[33] Hand, *The Bill of Rights*, 69–70 (1958).

[34] *id.*, 74.

[35] In *Dennis v. U.S.*, 341 U.S., 494, 525 (1951).

[36] Griswold, 'Felix Frankfurter – Teacher of the Law', 76 *Harv. L. Rev.*, 7, 12 (1962).

[37] Reich, 'Mr. Justice Black and the Living Constitution', 76 *Harv. L. Rev.*, 673, 742 (1963).

[38] *id.*, at 743.

[39] *id.*, at 742.

[40] Black, 'The Bill of Rights', 35 *N.Y.U.L. Rev.*, 865, 879 (1960).

[41] Meiklejohn, 'The First Amendment is an Absolute', 1961 *Supreme Court Review*, 245 (Kurland ed.).

[41a] For a discussion of the role of factual considerations in *ad hoc* balancing, see Emerson, 'Toward a General Theory of the First Amendment', 72 *Yale L. J.*, 854, 912 (1963); see also n. 22, ch. V *supra.*, for literature on 'consequences'.

[42] Mendelson, *Justices Black and Frankfurter: Conflict in Court* (1961).

[43] McKay, 'The Preference for Freedom', 34 *N.Y.U.L. Rev.*, 1182, 1193-1203 (1959).

[44] Hook, *The Paradoxes of Freedom*, 55 (1962).

[45] Sartre, *L'Existentialisme est un Humanisme*, 89-90 (1960 ed.), my translation.

[46] See n. 9, ch. III *supra*. On consistency see Schick, 'Consistency', 75 *Phil. Rev.*, 467 (1966); see generally, Williams, 'Consistency and Realism', 40 Sup. Vol. *Aristotelian Soc'y*, 1 (1966), and 'Consistency in Ethics', a symposium in 39 Sup. Vol. *Aristotelian Soc'y*, 103 f. (1965).

[46a] For a broad perspective on recent writings, see VII *Nomos, Rational Decision* (1965), and Bennett, *Rationality* (1964), as well as Blanshard, *Reason and Analysis* (1962). See also Barry, *Political Argument* (1965), Bartley, *The Retreat to Commitment* (1962), Winch, *The Idea of a Social Science* (1958), and Perelman, 'What the Philosopher May Learn From the Study of Law', 11 *Natural L. Forum*, 1 (1966), as well as his *Of Justice and the Problem of Argument* (1963), see also Polanyi, *Personal Knowledge* (1958), and Aiken, *Reason and Conduct* (1962). Note also, Pole, *Conditions of Rational Inquiry* (1961), and Crawshay-Williams, *Methods and Criteria of Reasoning* (1957).

INDEX

GEORGE ALLEN & UNWIN LTD

London: 40 Museum Street, W.C.1

Auckland: P.O. Box 36013, Northcote Central, N.4
Barbados: P.O. Box 222, Bridgetown
Beirut: Deeb Building, Jeanne d'Arc Street
Bombay: 15 Graham Road, Ballard Estate, Bombay 1
Buenos Aires: Escritorio 454–459, Florida 165
Calcutta: 17 Chittaranjan Avenue, Calcutta 13
Cape Town: 68 Shortmarket Street
Hong Kong: 105 Wing On Mansion, 26 Hancow Road, Kowloon
Ibadan: P.O. Box 62
Karachi: Karachi Chambers, McLeod Road
Madras: Mohan Mansions, 38c Mount Road, Madras 6
Mexico: Villalongin 32–10, Piso, Mexico 5, D.F.
Nairobi: P.O. Box 4536
New Delhi: 13–14 Asaf Ali Road, New Delhi 1
Ontario: 81 Curlew Drive, Don Mills
São Paulo: Caixa Postal 8675
Singapore: 36c Prinsep Street, Singapore 7
Sydney, N.S.W.: Bradbury House, 55 York Street
Tokyo: P.O. Box 26, Kamata

MAN IN SEARCH OF HIMSELF
JEAN CHARON

Taking George Breuil's grim jest that, as the twentieth century progresses, man is reverting to the cave, the author strives to show how the intellectual caveman can break free from his den.

He develops the theory that in the study of his psychic make-up we shall find a better understanding of man's true vocation in the cosmos, that by modelling ourselves upon Einstein's methods of General Relativity, we can produce a field language for the study of 'the mechanisms of life'. He discusses Teilhard de Chardin, Kurt Gödel, Descartes, Max Planck, Einstein, Heisenberg, and Jung: delves into psychoanalysis: compares the languages of religion, science and art: embracing past, present and future, traces the processes of evolution till he sees 'a new humanity already on the horizon'.

Like Alexis Carrel the biologist thirty years ago, he is a specialist broken out of his cell; and as he bursts into this new world, he declares, 'I have seen landscapes often new to me, that filled me with wonder,' and like a flare lighting the night, his search of the universe illumines man.

M. Charon is well known in the scientific world for his *Eléments d'une Théorie Unitaire d'Universe* published in Paris and Geneva in 1962. He has also written *La Connaissance de l'Univers*, which won the Prix Nautilus, and *Du Temps, De l'Espace et des Hommes*.

PHILOSOPHICAL ESSAYS
BERTRAND RUSSELL

This volume is essentially a reprint of a book, with the same title, published in 1910. But because two essays in that volume have since been reprinted in *Mysticism and Logic*, they have been replaced by an article on history and another on Poincare's 'Science and Hypothesis'. Otherwise the essays stand exactly as originally published and the author has made no attempt to modify them to accord with changes in his opinions which have developed in the interval. The collection includes 'The Elements of Ethics', 'Pragmatism', 'The Monistic Theory of Truth', 'James' Conception of Truth' and 'On the Nature of Truth and Falsehood'.

PHILOSOPHY OF SPACE AND TIME

MICHAEL WHITEMAN

A mathematician who is also a mystic is exceptionally well qualified to survey the mysterious subject of space and time. Dr Whiteman, Associate Professor of Applied Mathematics at Cape Town University and author of *The Mystical Life*, brings the mathematician's detachment and the mystic's insight to this book and presents the most thorough treatment of space and time yet seen. For the expert he provides an indispensable textbook likely to stand unchallenged for many years; for the intelligent layman, an opening into an absorbing field of knowledge, in a world where religious beliefs about the nature of the universe have lost their authority, but interest in the infinite is at its greatest.

Special topics include analysis of perception and measurement, 'the sixfold space-conceptuality', varieties of time awareness and control, interpretation of the theory of relativity and quantum theory, cosmological measurement and representation, and a critique of philosophies of nature from A.D. 1600 to the present day.

Dr Whiteman has published papers on Relativity, Philosophy of Science, Psychical Research, Comparative Religion and Mysticism, and has been lecturing on relativity and quantum theory since 1946 at Cape Town.

PHILOSOPHY OF WHITEHEAD

W. MAYS

Whitehead stands out among modern philosophers by his depth of vision and wide range of interests. This book effectively demonstrates that his thought has a much greater consistency and precision than is usually assumed . The author convincingly argues that the key to the understanding of Whitehead's philosophical system is to be found rather in his earlier philosophy of science than in traditional philosophy. He contends that logical mathematical and physical ideas, as well as descriptions of direct experience, play an essential role in Whitehead's later thought. On the one hand, this book gives a critical exposition of the main concepts of Whitehead's philosophy as seen in their scientific perspective. On the other, it clarifies his treatment of specific philosophical problems, such as the nature of sense-perception, causality, free-will and the body-mind problem. In this way the author throws a new light on those features of Whitehead's system which have puzzled philosophers for three decades.

PHILOSOPHY AND RELIGION
AXEL HÄGERSTRÖM

During the first half of the twentieth century an anti-metaphysical philosophy grew up at Uppsala University in Sweden. The founder of the movement was Axel Hägerström, although the development of its distinctive ideas was the composite achievement of a number of extremely capable philosophers, not the least of whom was Adolf Phalen.

The Uppsala philosophy had a profound impact on Swedish thought, which has become almost universally anti-metaphysical in the twentieth century. American and British positivism, however, was all but oblivious to the Scandinavian movement. This failure of communication was especially unfortunate from the Anglo-American side, for the approach of the Swedish positivists was much more judicious than that of the Vienna circle. The Swedish philosophers might have shown how positivism could avoid the mistakes which have brought it into general disrepute.

A PHILOSOPHER'S PILGRIMAGE
ALBAN WIDGERY

This is the record of the life of a philosopher who never allowed concern with ideas to distract him from the richness of particular experiences. He was a student, colleague and friend of some of the leading personalities of the last half century. Having lived in England, Scotland, Germany, France, India, Hawaii and the United States, he formed definite impressions of their peoples. In India, on the personal staff of H.H. Sayaji Rao III, he greatly influenced him in his pioneer achievements. Associated with Hindus, Buddhists, Parsis, Muslims and Jews, he came to appreciate essentials of their faiths. He critically considered the teachings of such thinkers as Nietzsche, Tolstoy and Shaw. With a clarity of exposition and with humour he presents a philosophy of life worthy of serious consideration.

GEORGE ALLEN & UNWIN LTD